Healthy
Vegetarian Cooking

HEALTHY VEGETARIAN COOKING

Innovative Vegetarian Recipes for the Adventurous Cook

Edited by Janet Swarbrick

CHARTWELL
BOOKS, INC.

Published in 2003 by Chartwell Books
A Division of Book Sales, Inc.
114 Northfield Avenue
Edison, New Jersey 08837

This edition produced for sale in the U.S.A., its
territories, and dependencies only.

A QUINTET BOOK

ISBN 0-7858-1730-1

This book was designed and produced by
Quintet Publishing Limited
6 Blundell Street
London N7 9BH

Designer: Isobel Gillan
Project Editor: Anna Briffa

Creative Director: Richard Dewing
Publisher: Oliver Salzmann

Typeset in Great Britain by
Central Southern Typesetters, Eastbourne
Manufactured in Singapore by
Eray Scan (Pte) Ltd.
Printed in Singapore by
Star Standard Industries (Pte) Ltd.

CONTENTS

INTRODUCTION

There is now such a selection of fruits, vegetables, and legumes in almost every supermarket, greengrocers or farm shop, be it in the center of the city or way out in the country! Given this astonishing variety it is quite easy to see that, for anyone wishing to follow a vegetarian diet, there is a wealth of ingredients readily available to provide colorful dishes of varied tastes and textures. In short, the modern vegetarian diet is fresh and exciting – no wonder more and more people are enjoying healthy, high fiber vegetarian eating.

Yet vegetarianism is not a new culinary trend – it was a way of life for many of the great thinkers and philosophers of the Ancient World, and has been advocated for thousands of years by sects of both the Hindu and Buddhist faiths, for whom all animal life is considered sacred.

A diet for a healthy world

Religion had great influence on all areas of people's lives for many centuries and, while it still does for some, it is now as likely to be emotional or environmental issues that make people stop and think about their diet as much as matters of spirituality.

Many teenagers turn to vegetarianism, largely due to peer pressure but also because the realisation that the lambs and piglets seen enjoying the sunshine are destined for the table. The lack of detailed answers to questions arising from intensive farming methods, notably the BSE crisis in Europe, has also persuaded many to embrace vegetarianism.

LEFT A diet rich in fresh vegetables is highly recommended.

Vegetarian or Vegan?

Many people refer to themselves as vegetarians if they do not eat red meat, but this is inaccurate. No vegetarians eat any animal flesh, which includes poultry and fish as well as red and white meats. Vegans, those who follow the strictest vegetarian diet, will not eat anything at all that is derived from animals – no cheese, butter or any milk-based foods; indeed some also refuse honey, which they do not believe should be taken from the bees. A creative vegan diet is one of the great culinary challenges.

Lacto-vegetarians do not eat any foods that involve the slaughter of animals, so they will not eat eggs although they do include dairy products such as cheese and milk, whereas octo-lacto vegetarians will eat eggs.

There are growing numbers of would-be vegetarians who eat fish. This is especially true of those who lead a very active life, or who are just converting to vegetarianism. Colloquially referred to as "demi-veg," this is a compromise in terms of true vegetarianism but one which many parents are happy to accept for their young people.

A healthy vegetarian diet

Many so called "modern" or Western diseases are inevitably linked to our over-processed, fatty convenience diet. Life-style also plays a large part in such illnesses. Fatty foods and lack of exercise undoubtedly contribute to heart disease, whereas a shortage of dietary fiber leads to many digestive disorders and diseases.

Animals are not the only source of dietary protein – cereals, nuts, and beans all contain secondary, or vegetable, proteins. Very few, however, contain all the essential amino acids necessary to recreate the protein that we eat as body protein. It is therefore of paramount importance that a vegetarian diet should be varied, incorporating all types of cereals and beans. The classic example of this is that bread made from wheat flour is incomplete in terms of essential amino acids – toast it and put a helping of baked beans on top and you have a protein-rich snack!

Fiber – the key to healthy eating

Fiber is the most important part of the vegetarian diet, the most effective weapon against the malaise brought on by the mediocrity of processed foods. Dietary fiber forms the cell walls of plants – the super-structure or skeleton. It is unique to plants and it is therefore easy to see that a diet rich in animal proteins and fat, but lacking in cereals and vegetables can be almost totally lacking in fiber – but why should this matter.

Fiber is essential for the efficient working of the digestive system and therefore the processing of our food.

A pappy diet is easy to eat and presents little intestinal challenge. Indeed, much of the progress in the early days of the "food industry" was aimed at making eating "easier" by refining foods. However, intestinal inactivity causes disorders and disease. In the less developed countries of the world where the staple diet is rice, lentils, and vegetables there is disease, but much of it is associated with vitamin deficiencies rather than with a lack of dietary fiber.

To keep healthy it is important to cook with, and eat, as many unprocessed foods as possible, which leads inevitably to a high fiber diet. What is amazing is that, even among meat-eaters, the foods that we think of as starches or carbohydrates (fiber foods) often contribute a significant amount of protein to the diet – between 20 and 30 percent of the protein in an average diet comes from potatoes. Cut out the animal proteins, which automatically leads to a reduction in fat, increase fiber-rich foods and a healthy diet is easily achieved.

Extra proteins for vegetarians

Vegetable protein foods are becoming more and more common, and there is quite a movement in agriculture towards soy, a high protein crop which can be used as solids or liquid and which produces a much better protein yield per acre than livestock. This is regarded as one of the most plausible ways of increasing the quality of the international diet.

Tofu, a recent introduction to many Westerners but a staple protein food of the Chinese for many thousands of years, also has a valuable place in the vegetarian diet. It is bean curd and is also known as soybean curd. It is best fresh when the texture is firm. Natural or smoked tofu may be sliced and quickly fried, then added to salads and other vegetable dishes, or beaten into fillings for pies and flans.

Other vegetable protein foods are being developed as chopped, sausage-like chunks to resemble meat. They often have little flavor of their own, but readily absorb flavorsome marinades and sauces. Combining these with foil-baked squashes and corns makes a vegetarian barbecue so much more interesting than the average meat-eaters feast of burnt sausages and chicken pieces.

Robust flavors for robust foods

Many beans and legumes respond deliciously to clever and inventive use of herbs and spices. Roasting your own whole spices, such as cumin and coriander seeds, in a dry skillet and grinding them just before use achieves the best possible flavor. Alternatively, buy small quantities of ground spices and replace them regularly. Dried seasonings are only at their best for a few months and certainly cease to pack a punch after a year.

Fresh herbs have the best flavor, but they can be very expensive, especially if you have to buy them from a supermarket. Keep freeze-dried herbs for emergencies but, if you are lucky enough to have a herb garden, do try to use fresh leaves whenever possible. Herbs for garnish should be chopped and added at the last moment, to retain both color and immediacy of flavor. Even if you do not have a garden it is a good idea to grow some herbs in pots on your windowsill – some varieties, such as basil, are indeed better this way than outside in an unreliable climate.

One of the most exciting trends in popular cooking in the last few years has been the use of salsas as salad garnishes, and these work especially well with bean-based dishes. A mixture as simple as an orange, tomatoes, scallions and roasted mustard seeds with cilantro and a chopped chile can add the most exciting explosion of color, texture, and flavor to a casserole or bake.

Cutting down on fat

You should never aim to eradicate fat from your diet completely as it is essential for a healthy skin, for energy and to keep the organs of the body "well-oiled" by providing a protective coating. Too much fat, however, causes problems – it is one of the food groups that can, unfortunately, be stored if we eat too much!

The benefits of fruit as a substitute for refined fatty desserts are numerous. Not only do they have no fat, but they supply essential vitamins, minerals, and fiber.

There is a certain amount of fat present in most foods, but especially in animal proteins. Cheese is a very concentrated fatty food and it is better to use less of a mature cheese than a larger amount of a mild one. It is essential not to be tempted to eat cheese two or three times a day – there are plenty of other ways of adding flavor to dishes, and many other foods that can be used for sandwich fillings and snacks.

Vegetarians often use nuts, but these contain large amounts of oil and therefore fat. Recipes that call for browned or fried nuts should be adapted to dry-frying nuts in a non-stick pan, or grilling them, so that extra oil is not required during cooking.

The use of plenty of fresh herbs can adequately compensate for any loss of dairy flavor in a healthy diet.

Fats for flavor

Fats, which include soft and solid spreads and oils, can be divided into three categories: *saturated fats* which are normally hard at room temperature and are mainly derived from meat or meat products, although coconut oil and palm oil also fall into this category. These fats tend to raise the blood cholesterol level above that which is required for healthy tissues and hormones, leading to atherosclerosis and possible heart attack.

Polyunsaturated fats are usually vegetable products, liquid at room temperature and which have a neutral effect on cholesterol. They include the most common vegetable oils, and the soft margarines which are clearly labeled as polyunsaturated, e.g. sunflower.

Monounsaturated fats are the group that has received most publicity in recent years as olive oil is a key member of the group. Avocados and peanut oil also fall into this group, which has been found to have a neutralising, beneficial effect on cholesterol in the blood.

It is therefore reasonable to suggest that olive oil is good for you and should be included in a healthy diet. It is not, however, an invitation to drown all foods in this delicious nectar which is still a fat and contains plenty of calories.

Stir-frying for health

Gone are the days of kids being packed off to college with a microwave cooker – now they want a wok! Stir-fries are cheap and filling, incorporating a good variety of colorful, crisp vegetables and spicy sauces, all cooked in just a spoonful or two or oil. The secret of a good stir-fry is to have all the ingredients ready, cut into similar-sized pieces, before you begin cooking. Heat the wok until hot, add a little oil and then the vegetables. Stir for two to three minutes, then serve with rice or noodles.

Treats and variety

Just because a pudding or cake is made with fiber-rich ingredients, doesn't make it healthy. Many such foods have a high proportion of fats and sugars and are absolutely loaded with calories. We all want treats occasionally, but where an active teenager will be able to devour these foods without adding an inch to the waistline, for most of us even high-fiber treats will have an unfortunate effect on the figure, and should be kept for special occasions only.

A healthy vegetarian diet is colorful, creative, and fun. Dare to try your own exotic combinations of foods and push the boundaries of conventionality by combining salads, salsas, and flavorings with robust and satisfying casseroles and bakes. And remember, a healthy diet is a varied diet, so enjoy experimenting with the enormous variety of fresh and dried foods that are now available.

FAT AND CHOLESTEROL CONTENT OF FOODS

	fat g PER 100g	cholesterol mg PER 100g
Milk and Milk Products		
Milk, cows'		
fresh, whole	3.8	14
long-life	3.8	14
fresh, skimmed	0.1	2
Milk, goats'	4.5	–
Cream		
light	21.2	66
heavy	35.0	100
Cheese		
Camembert-type	23.2	72
Cheddar-type	33.5	70
Cheddar-type, low-fat, average	16.0	varies
Cheddar-type, with sunflower oil	33.0	more than 5
cottage cheese, low-fat	4.0	13
cream cheese, full fat	47.4	94
Yogurt, low fat		
plain	1.0	7
fruit	1.0	6
Fats and Oils		
butter, salted	82.0	70
lard	99.0	70
low-fat spread	40.7	trace
margarine, hard	81.0	varies
margarine, sunflower oil	80.0	less than 5
vegetable oils	99.9	trace
Eggs		
whole , raw	10.9	450
white, raw	trace	0
yolk, raw	30.5	1260
dried	43.3	1780

BREAKFAST

Breakfast Crunch

Honey-poached Figs

Oat Pancakes

Broiled Fruits with Honey

Grapefruit Cocktail

Apricot Granola

Banana Cocktail

Spicy Potato Cakes

BREAKFAST CRUNCH

SERVES 6

¼ cup sunflower seeds

¼ cup pine nuts

¼ cup sesame seeds

2 oranges

2 tbsp brown sugar

½ cup dried figs, chopped

2 large bananas

2½ cups low-fat yogurt

≈ Using a dry skillet, roast the sunflower seeds and pine nuts for 3 minutes over a moderate heat, then add the sesame seeds and roast for a further 3 minutes, stirring to give even browning. Remove the pan from the heat.

≈ Coarsely grate the peel from 1 orange and add to the pan with the sugar and dried figs. Stir until well combined and cook for 2 minutes. Leave to cool.

≈ Remove the peel and pith from the oranges and cut them into pieces. Slice the bananas and mix with the oranges and yogurt, divide among four dishes and top each with the fig mixture. Serve at once.

NUTRITION FACTS	
Amount per Serving	
Calories 291	Calories from Fat 126
	% Daily Value
Total Fat 14g	21%
Saturated Fat 2g	10%
Polyunsaturated Fat 7g	0%
Monounsaturated Fat 4g	0%
Cholesterol 3mg	1%
Sodium 82mg	3%
Total Carbohydrate 34g	11%
Dietary Fiber 5g	20%
Sugars 32g	0%
Protein 10g	0%

Percent daily values are based on a 2000 calorie diet

HONEY-POACHED FIGS

SERVES 4

1 cinnamon stick

3 tbsp clear honey

1 cup water or orange juice

2½ cups semi-dried figs

1 cup plain low-fat yogurt

≈ Put the cinnamon stick, honey, and water or orange juice into a shallow pan and bring to a boil. Add the figs and simmer for 20 minutes, turning them occasionally. Remove from the heat and set aside to cool.

≈ Lift out the figs with a slotted spoon. Stir the yogurt into the poaching liquid, blending it thoroughly. Pour into a serving bowl and stir in the figs.

NUTRITION FACTS	
Amount per Serving	
Calories 262	Calories from Fat 18
	% Daily Value
Total Fat 2g	3%
Saturated Fat 0.2g	1%
Polyunsaturated Fat 0g	0%
Monounsaturated Fat 0.1g	0%
Cholesterol 2mg	0.6%
Sodium 100mg	4%
Total Carbohydrate 59g	20%
Dietary Fiber 10g	40%
Sugars 59g	0%
Protein 6g	0%

Percent daily values are based on a 2000 calorie diet

OAT PANCAKES

SERVES 4

Oat pancakes, like any others, freeze well, so it is a good idea to make a double batch and store some of them.

⅓ cup rolled oats

⅓ cup (generous) whole wheat-flour

pinch salt

1 tsp grated orange rind

⅝ cup orange juice

⅝ cup skimmed milk

2 egg whites, lightly beaten

oil, for brushing

2 tbsp light unrefined brown sugar

Filling

1 cup low-fat cottage cheese

1¼ cup seedless raisins

1 tsp grated orange rind

Garnish

orange sections

≈ In a bowl, mix together the oats, flour, salt, and orange rind. Gradually pour on the orange juice and milk, beating constantly. Fold in the egg whites. Lightly brush a non-stick omelet pan with oil, and heat it over medium heat. Pour in just enough of the batter to cover the base.

≈ Cook the pancake until it bubbles and is browned on the under side. Flip or toss it and cook on the other side.

≈ Cook the remainder of the batter in the same way. The mixture makes 8–10 pancakes.

≈ Mix together the cheese, raisins, and orange rind for the filling. Spread about 2 tablespoons of the mixture in the center of each pancake and roll them up. You can prepare the pancakes to this stage, cover, and store in the refrigerator overnight.

≈ Set the broiler to medium. Arrange the pancakes in a flame-proof dish, and sprinkle them with the sugar. Broil until the sugar caramelizes, then serve hot, decorated with the orange sections.

NUTRITION FACTS	
Amount per Serving	
Calories 350	Calories from Fat 36
	% Daily Value
Total Fat 4g	6%
Saturated Fat 2g	10%
Polyunsaturated Fat 1g	0%
Monounsaturated Fat 1g	0%
Cholesterol 8mg	3%
Sodium 304mg	13%
Total Carbohydrate 69g	23%
Dietary Fiber 4g	16%
Sugars 56g	0%
Protein 14g	0%

Percent daily values are based on a 2000 calorie diet

BROILED FRUITS WITH HONEY

SERVES 4

P̲resent citrus fruits in a different way — broiled and served piping hot in a golden honey sauce.

2 grapefruits, peeled and sectioned

3 oranges, peeled and sectioned

6 tbsp clear honey

2 tbsp brown unrefined sugar

1 tbsp polyunsaturated margarine

Garnish

2 tbsp chopped mint

≈ Place the grapefruit and orange segments in a single layer in a flameproof dish.

≈ In a small pan, heat the honey, sugar, and margarine until it has melted. Stir to blend it well, and pour it over the fruit.

≈ Broil the fruit for about 4 minutes, until the sections are just beginning to brown and the sauce is bubbling. Sprinkle with the mint and serve at once. Chilled plain low-fat yogurt makes a good accompaniment.

NUTRITION FACTS	
Amount per Serving	
Calories 237	Calories from Fat 27
	% Daily Value
Total Fat 3g	5%
Saturated Fat 1g	5%
Polyunsaturated Fat 1g	0%
Monounsaturated Fat 1g	0%
Cholesterol 0mg	0%
Sodium 42mg	1.8%
Total Carbohydrate 53g	18%
Dietary Fiber 5.5g	22%
Sugars 53g	0%
Protein 2.5g	0%

Percent daily values are based on a 2000 calorie diet

GRAPEFRUIT COCKTAIL

SERVES 4

As for other citrus fruit, grapefruit is believed to slow down the rate at which sugar is metabolized. Here the fruit is transformed into a lively cocktail to start the day or begin a meal.

2 large juicy grapefruit

4 oz seedless green grapes

2 kiwi fruit, peeled, halved and sliced

4 mint sprigs

≈ Peel the grapefruit and remove all the pith. Hold the fruit over a basin and use a sharp serrated knife to cut in towards the middle of the fruit, removing the fleshy segments and leaving behind the membranes that separate them. Catch all the juice.

≈ Leave small grapes whole or halve larger ones and mix them with the grapefruit. Add the kiwi fruit and mint, then mix lightly.

NUTRITION FACTS	
Amount per Serving	
Calories 72	Calories from Fat 5
	% Daily Value
Total Fat 0.5g	0.8%
Saturated Fat 0g	0%
Polyunsaturated Fat 0g	0%
Monounsaturated Fat 0g	0%
Cholesterol 0mg	0%
Sodium 6mg	0.25%
Total Carbohydrate 17g	6%
Dietary Fiber 1.5g	6%
Sugars 17g	0%
Protein 1.5g	0%
Percent daily values are based on a 2000 calorie diet	

APRICOT GRANOLA

SERVES 8

You can vary the granola mixture in many ways, substituting different nuts and seeds and using other dried fruits in place of the apricots. Do not store the granola until it has completely cooled, or it will sweat and the ingredients will soften.

3 tbsp sunflower oil

6 tbsp clear honey

1 cup rolled oats

⅔ cup rolled jumbo oats

⅓ cup hazelnuts, chopped

⅛ cup sunflower seeds

⅛ cup raisins

1 cup dried apricots, chopped

≈ Set the oven to 325°F. Melt the oil and the honey in a saucepan over a low heat. Stir in the oats, chopped nuts, and seeds, mix well, and immediately remove from the heat.

≈ Spread the mixture on a cookie sheet and bake in the oven for 25 minutes, stirring from time to time with a wooden spoon.

≈ Remove the cookie sheet from the oven, stir in the chopped apricots, and set aside to cool. When the mixture has cooled thoroughly, store it in an airtight jar in the refrigerator.

≈ You can serve the granola with a tempting variety of dairy products and fruit juices. Try it with buttermilk, or plain low-fat yogurt mixed half-and-half with orange, apple, or pineapple juice, or with fruit juice alone.

NUTRITION FACTS	
Amount per Serving	
Calories 194	Calories from Fat 80
	% Daily Value
Total Fat 9g	14%
Saturated Fat 1g	5%
Polyunsaturated Fat 4g	0%
Monounsaturated Fat 4g	0%
Cholesterol 0mg	0%
Sodium 11mg	0.5%
Total Carbohydrate 26g	9%
Dietary Fiber 4g	16%
Sugars 13g	0%
Protein 4g	0%
Percent daily values are based on a 2000 calorie diet	

BANANA COCKTAIL

SERVES 4

This is a nourishing "spoon drink" to serve to someone who's in a hurry.

1⅓ cup rolled oats

¾ cup skimmed milk

4 tbsp clear honey

2 large eating apples, peeled, cored, and grated

2 medium bananas, thinly sliced

juice of 1 lemon

juice of 1 orange

2 tsp grated orange rind

1¼ cup plain low-fat yogurt

Garnish

4 tsp dark Muscovado or brown sugar

2 tbsp fresh or frozen berries, or orange sections

NUTRITION FACTS	
Amount per Serving	
Calories 328	Calories from Fat 27

	% Daily Value
Total Fat 3g	5%
Saturated Fat 1g	5%
Polyunsaturated Fat 1g	0%
Monounsaturated Fat 1g	0%
Cholesterol 4mg	1.3%
Sodium 98mg	4%
Total Carbohydrate 70g	23%
Dietary Fiber 5g	20%
Sugars 53g	0%
Protein 9g	0%

Percent daily values are based on a 2000 calorie diet

≈ Soak the oats in skimmed milk overnight. In the morning stir in all the remaining ingredients, and divide the mixture among four individual serving glasses, such as sundae glasses.

≈ Sprinkle 1 teaspoon of sugar over each glass, and decorate it with whatever fruit is available. Scottish oatcakes, available from some specialty stores, make a very good accompaniment.

SPICY POTATO CAKES

SERVES 4

If you prepare the spicy potato cake mixture in advance, it can be cooked quickly the next morning in a non-stick pan. The pancakes are especially good served with broiled tomatoes.

≈ Soak the potatoes in cold water for about 30 minutes to remove some of the starch. Drain, rinse, and dry them, and then grate coarsely into a bowl.

≈ Stir in the flour, bran flakes, onion, parsley, and curry powder to taste, and season with salt. Lastly, stir in the milk and shape the mixture into a round. Separate it into 8 equal-sized pieces.

· Brush your hands with flour, and shape the pieces into flat rounds. Sprinkle the potato cakes with whole-wheat flour to cover them on all sides.

· ≈ Lightly brush a non-stick skillet with oil, and heat it over a medium heat. Fry the potato cakes for 4–5 minutes on each side, until they are evenly brown.

· Serve them hot, garnished with parsley.

1½ lb potatoes, peeled or scraped

2 tbsp whole-wheat flour, plus extra for dusting

2 tbsp 100% bran cereal, crushed

1 small onion, grated

2 tbsp chopped parsley

1–2 tsp curry powder

salt

3 tbsp low-fat milk

oil, for brushing

Garnish

parsley sprigs

NUTRITION FACTS	
Amount per Serving	
Calories 176	Calories from Fat 9
	% Daily Value
Total Fat 1g	1.5%
Saturated Fat 0.1g	0.5%
Polyunsaturated Fat 0.3g	0%
Monounsaturated Fat 0g	0%
Cholesterol 0mg	0%
Sodium 51mg	2%
Total Carbohydrate 39g	13%
Dietary Fiber 6g	24%
Sugars 3g	0%
Protein 6g	0%

Percent daily values are based on a 2000 calorie diet

APPETIZERS, SOUPS, AND SALADS

EASTERN PASTA SALAD

SERVES 4

A traditional combination of mint and lemon makes this dish a salad for summer. Choose your favorite pasta shapes for this recipe, and serve with warm pita bread to mop up the delicious dressing.

¾ lb dried pasta shells

dash of olive oil

14 oz can garbanzo beans, drained

4 tbsp chopped, fresh mint

finely grated zest of 1 lemon

For the dressing

3 cloves of garlic, crushed

4 tbsp extra virgin olive oil

3 tbsp white-wine vinegar

freshly squeezed juice of 1 lemon

salt and freshly ground black pepper

≈ Bring a large saucepan of water to a boil, and add the pasta with a dash of olive oil. Cook for about 10 minutes, stirring occasionally, until tender. Drain and rinse under cold running water. Drain again, and place in a large mixing bowl.

≈ Add the garbanzo beans, mint, and lemon zest to the pasta. Place all the dressing ingredients in a screw-top jar, and shake well to mix. Pour the dressing over the garbanzo beans and mix well to combine. Cover, and chill for at least 30 minutes. Toss before serving.

NUTRITION FACTS

Amount per Serving

Calories 528	Calories from Fat 144
	% Daily Value
Total Fat 16g	25%
Saturated Fat 2.5g	12.5%
Polyunsaturated Fat 3g	0%
Monounsaturated Fat 9g	0%
Cholesterol 0mg	0%
Sodium 230mg	10%
Total Carbohydrate 83g	28%
Dietary Fiber 10g	40%
Sugars 2g	0%
Protein 18g	0%

Percent daily values are based on a 2000 calorie diet

BORSCHT

SERVES 6

Quintessentially Russian, borscht is a fresh-tasting, healthy soup which can be served hot or cold depending on the occasion. Beet is a naturally sweet vegetable, and gives the soup a unique flavor.

2 large onions

3 large beets

3 large carrots

2 parsnips

4 stalks celery

3 tbsp tomato paste

4 large tomatoes

½ small white cabbage, shredded

1 tbsp honey

1 tbsp lemon juice

salt and freshly ground black pepper

handful of chopped parsley

all-purpose white flour

low-fat sour cream or yogurt

≈ Cut onions, beet, carrots, parsnips, and celery into matchsticks. Bring a large pan of salted water to a boil, add the tomato paste and the vegetables and simmer for 30 minutes until tender.

≈ Skin the tomatoes, remove the seeds, and chop. Add to the pan with the cabbage, honey, lemon juice, and seasoning. Simmer for 5 minutes, then throw in a handful of chopped parsley. Check seasoning.

≈ If necessary, thicken the soup with a blend of a little flour and low-fat sour cream. The soup is best made the day before it is to be eaten. Reheat and serve with a bowl of low-fat sour cream or yogurt.

NUTRITION FACTS	
Amount per Serving	
Calories 97	Calories from Fat 9
	% Daily Value
Total Fat 1g	1.5%
Saturated Fat 0.3g	1.5%
Polyunsaturated Fat 0.4g	0%
Monounsaturated Fat 0.3g	0%
Cholesterol 1mg	0.3%
Sodium 76mg	3%
Total Carbohydrate 19g	6%
Dietary Fiber 6g	24%
Sugars 15g	0%
Protein 4g	0%

Percent daily values are based on a 2000 calorie diet

NUTTY CUCUMBER BOATS

SERVES 4

A perfect first course for a hot summer day, or for an outdoor meal. You could add texture and flavor – fiber too – by mixing 2 tablespoons of seedless raisins into the filling.

8-inch piece cucumber, cut in half
    lengthwise
⅓ cup pine nuts toasted
½ cup cottage cheese
4 medium tomatoes, skinned,
    seeded, and chopped
2 tsp chopped dill
1 tsp chopped mint

Garnish
lettuce leaves
dill sprigs

Do not mix the filling more than a few minutes before serving, or the nuts will become soggy and lose their crispness.

≈ Scoop out the centers of the cucumber pieces and cut into 2-inch pieces.

≈ A few minutes before serving mix together the nuts, cheese, tomatoes, dill, and mint. Spoon into each cucumber wedge.

≈ Arrange the cucumber "boats" on a bed of lettuce leaves, garnish with dill sprigs and serve at once.

NUTRITION FACTS	
Amount per Serving	
Calories 102	Calories from Fat 63
	% Daily Value
Total Fat 7g	11%
Saturated Fat 1g	5%
Polyunsaturated Fat 4g	0%
Monounsaturated Fat 2g	0%
Cholesterol 3mg	1%
Sodium 105mg	4%
Total Carbohydrate 4g	1%
Dietary Fiber 2g	8%
Sugars 4g	0%
Protein 6g	0%

Percent daily values are based on a 2000 calorie diet

CREAMY GARLIC MUSHROOMS

SERVES 4

These are perfect baked-potato fillers!

2 tbsp olive oil

1 large garlic clove, crushed

2 scallions, chopped

salt and freshly ground black pepper

12 oz button mushrooms

6 oz low-fat soft cheese

a little parsley, chopped (optional)

≈ Heat the oil in a large skillet. Add the garlic, scallions, and seasoning, and cook for 2 minutes. Then add all the mushrooms and toss them over high heat for a couple of minutes, until they are hot. Do not cook the mushrooms until their juices run as they will be too watery.

≈ Clear a space (like a well) in the middle of the mushrooms, add the soft cheese and stir it for a few seconds, until it begins to soften. Gradually mix all the mushrooms with the cheese until they are evenly coated.

≈ Divide among individual plates or dishes and top with a little chopped parsley if desired. Serve at once with warmed whole-wheat bread or toast.

≈ Alternatively, transfer the mushrooms to a bowl, cool, then cover and chill them briefly before serving.

NUTRITION FACTS	
Amount per Serving	
Calories 141	Calories from Fat 108
	% Daily Value
Total Fat 12g	18%
Saturated Fat 5g	25%
Polyunsaturated Fat 1g	0%
Monounsaturated Fat 6g	0%
Cholesterol 18mg	6%
Sodium 5mg	0.2%
Total Carbohydrate 2g	0.6%
Dietary Fiber 1.5g	6%
Sugars 2g	0%
Protein 6g	0%

Percent daily values are based on a 2000 calorie diet

TOMATO AND BASIL SALAD

SERVES 4

Take advantage of the ripe tomatoes and surplus of basil from summer gardens with this cool and elegant – but simple – salad. Drizzle your favorite low-fat dressing on top.

4 large ripe tomatoes, sliced
bunch of fresh basil
4–6 thin slices of red onion
salt to taste
freshly ground black pepper
low-fat mozzarella-type cheese

≈ Slice the tomatoes, salt lightly, and let them drain on paper towels for about 20 minutes.
≈ Wash the basil and dry well with paper towels or in a salad spinner. Tear the leaves from the stems and arrange a thin layer of leaves on a platter. Top with about half the tomato slices. Separate the onion rings and scatter about half over the tomatoes. Add another layer of basil, tomatoes and onions. Sprinkle lightly with freshly-ground black pepper, and garnish with a few extra basil leaves.
≈ A variation is to top the tomatoes with thin slices of the low-fat mozzarella-type cheese.

NUTRITION FACTS	
Amount per Serving	
Calories 52	Calories from Fat 22
	% Daily Value
Total Fat 2.5g	4%
Saturated Fat 1.5g	7.5%
Polyunsaturated Fat 0.3g	0%
Monounsaturated Fat 0.7g	0%
Cholesterol 7mg	2%
Sodium 71mg	3%
Total Carbohydrate 4g	1%
Dietary Fiber 2g	8%
Sugars 4g	0%
Protein 3.5g	0%

Percent daily values are based on a 2000 calorie diet

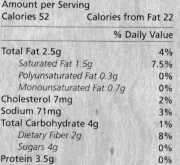

EGG AND OKRA SCRAMBLE

SERVES 2

4 oz okra

1 tbsp oil

⅓ cup chopped onion

¼ tsp cumin seeds

4 tbsp chopped tomato

pinch of turmeric

¼ tsp chili powder

½ tsp salt

freshly ground black pepper

2 tsp lemon juice

3 large eggs

3 cloves garlic, chopped

1 scallion, finely chopped

≈ Rinse and dry the okra well; top and tail each and then cut it into 3 to 4 slices.

≈ Heat the oil in a medium-sized nonstick skillet with a lid. Soften the onion, then add the cumin seeds.

≈ Add the okra, tomato, turmeric, chili powder, and half the salt. Stir, then let the vegetables cook in their own moisture by covering the pan with its lid, over a low heat for 10 to 12 minutes, until the okra is tender. Grind some black pepper over the pot and sprinkle in the lemon juice.

≈ Break the eggs into a bowl and beat with 2 tablespoons of water. Stir in the garlic, scallion, and the remaining salt.

≈ Pour the egg mixture over the vegetable mixture in the pan and, as soon as the eggs are lightly set, break up the mixture and continue to stir while it cooks. Serve immediately.

NUTRITION FACTS	
Amount per Serving	
Calories 221	Calories from Fat 144
	% Daily Value
Total Fat 16g	25%
Saturated Fat 3.5g	17.5%
Polyunsaturated Fat 5g	0%
Monounsaturated Fat 6g	0%
Cholesterol 357mg	119%
Sodium 139mg	6%
Total Carbohydrate 6g	2%
Dietary Fiber 4g	16%
Sugars 5g	0%
Protein 14g	0%

Percent daily values are based on a 2000 calorie diet

VEGETABLE SALAD

SERVES 6

In Scandinavia this salad known as rosolli *is very often eaten as a savory pick-me-up on Christmas Eve morning.*

7 fresh beets

5 potatoes

7 carrots

2 apples

2 medium onions

3 large sprigs fresh dill, or 1½ tsp dill seed

salt

low-fat mayonnaise (optional)

≈ Boil the beets and potatoes in their skins with the carrots until tender. Refrigerate for 2–3 hours.

≈ Peel and chop the cooked vegetables, apples, and onions, and chop the dill.

≈ Mix them all together, and season with salt, tossing a few times. Serve with low-fat mayonnaise.

NUTRITION FACTS		
Amount per Serving		
Calories 85		Calories from Fat 4
		% Daily Value
Total Fat 0.4g		0.6%
Saturated Fat 0.1g		0.5%
Polyunsaturated Fat 0.2g		0%
Monounsaturated Fat 0g		0%
Cholesterol 0mg		0%
Sodium 50mg		2%
Total Carbohydrate 19.5g		6.5%
Dietary Fiber 5g		20%
Sugars 13.5g		0%
Protein 2g		0%

Percent daily values are based on a 2000 calorie diet

SPICY MUSHROOM DIP

SERVES 4

1 clove garlic, crushed

1 tsp fresh ginger, ground

1 tsp fresh lemon grass, ground or
   grated lemon peel

1 tbsp chopped fresh cilantro

1 tbsp sesame oil

16 firm white mushrooms

Dipping Sauce

3 tbsp roasted peanuts

1 red chili pepper, finely chopped

1 clove garlic, minced

1 tbsp mint, finely chopped

1 tbsp lime or lemon juice

3 tbsp light soy sauce mixed with
   1 tsp anchovy paste

2 tbsp sesame oil

½ cup skimmed milk

≈ Mix the garlic, ginger, lemon grass, cilantro, and sesame oil. Marinate the mushrooms in the mixture for 3–4 hours, turning frequently.

≈ Make the dipping sauce by mixing and pounding all the dipping sauce ingredients together except for the skimmed milk. A rough paste should result. Stir in the skimmed milk.

≈ Thread the mushrooms onto four skewers. Place on the barbecue or under a high broiler for about 3 minutes on either side, basting with the marinade. Serve hot with the dipping sauce.

NUTRITION FACTS	
Amount per Serving	
Calories 137	Calories from Fat 108
	% Daily Value
Total Fat 12g	18%
Saturated Fat 2g	10%
Polyunsaturated Fat 5g	0%
Monounsaturated Fat 5g	0%
Cholesterol 1mg	0.3%
Sodium 345mg	14%
Total Carbohydrate 3g	1%
Dietary Fiber 1.5g	6%
Sugars 2g	0%
Protein 4g	0%

Percent daily values are based on a 2000 calorie diet

WELL-SEASONED MUSHROOMS

SERVES 4

Wonderful wild mushrooms are used here, but this dish is good even with cultivated ones. Serve with toasted bread.

2 lb mushrooms (preferably including portobello mushrooms), cleaned

1 large onion, finely chopped

2 tbsp olive oil

½ chili pepper, seeded and chopped or cayenne pepper to taste

2 garlic cloves, finely chopped

salt and freshly ground black pepper

2 fl oz dry white wine

2 tbsp brandy

2 tbsp chopped parsley

≈ Fry the onion in the oil in a large flameproof casserole, adding the garlic and chili or cayenne pepper once it has softened.

• ≈ Add the sliced mushrooms and fry until they soften. Season and add the wine and brandy. Cook further to reduce the liquid a little, sprinkle with parsley and serve.

NUTRITION FACTS	
Amount per Serving	
Calories 118	Calories from Fat 63
	% Daily Value
Total Fat 7g	11%
Saturated Fat 1g	5%
Polyunsaturated Fat 1g	0%
Monounsaturated Fat 4g	0%
Cholesterol 0mg	0%
Sodium 14mg	0.6%
Total Carbohydrate 3	1%
Dietary Fiber 1.5g	6%
Sugars 2g	0%
Protein 5g	0%

Percent daily values are based on a 2000 calorie diet

ITALIAN BEAN AND PASTA SOUP

SERVES 6

Bean soups are popular and seasonings vary but chunky, flavorful soups are always welcome as a first course or light meal. This Jewish-Italian soup is scented with sage, rosemary, and basil.

1½ cups dried navy or cannellini beans, soaked at least 8 hours

2 tbsp olive oil

1 onion, finely chopped

1 stalk celery, finely chopped

1 carrot, finely chopped

1 lb fresh tomatoes, peeled, seeded and chopped, or 2 8-oz cans plum tomatoes, drained and chopped

3–4 garlic cloves, peeled and crushed

2 vegetable bouillon cubes, crumbled

2 bay leaves

2 tsp dried rosemary, crumbled

1 tsp dried sage, crumbled

1 cup small pasta shapes, such as shells, bows, or wheels

3 tbsp chopped fresh parsley

3 tbsp shredded fresh basil leaves

salt and freshly ground black pepper

Garnish

fresh basil leaves

≈ Drain soaked beans. In a large Dutch oven or saucepan, combine beans and 1 quart water. Over high heat, bring to a boil. Skim off any foam which comes to the surface, reduce heat and simmer until beans are tender, 1 to 1½ hours. Add water occasionally so beans remain covered. Remove from heat.

≈ In another large saucepan, over medium heat, heat olive oil. Add chopped onion and cook until onion begins to soften, 4–5 minutes. Add chopped celery and chopped carrot and continue cooking 4–5 minutes longer. Add chopped tomatoes, garlic, bouillon cubes, bay leaves, rosemary, and sage and bring to a boil.

≈ Cook, uncovered, until vegetables are tender, about 5 minutes. Add cooked beans and 1 quart cooking liquid (make up liquid with water, if necessary).

≈ Bring soup to a boil. Add pasta and cook, uncovered, until pasta is tender, 8–10 minutes. Stir in chopped parsley and shredded basil. Season with salt and freshly ground black pepper. Garnish each portion with a fresh basil leaf.

NUTRITION FACTS

Amount per Serving

Calories 184	Calories from Fat 45
	% Daily Value
Total Fat 5g	8%
Saturated Fat 1g	5%
Polyunsaturated Fat 1g	0%
Monounsaturated Fat 3g	0%
Cholesterol 0mg	0%
Sodium 25mg	1%
Total Carbohydrate 29g	10%
Dietary Fiber 8g	32%
Sugars 5g	0%
Protein 8g	0%

Percent daily values are based on a 2000 calorie diet

CRUNCHY BEAN AND CORN APPETIZER

SERVES 4

This simple vegetable dish, which is presented with style, incorporates a wonderful blend of textures and flavors. It would also make an attractive salad dish for a cold buffet.

½ lb green beans, trimmed

1 cup canned corn, drained

salt and freshly ground black pepper

1 tsp chopped mint

1 tsp chopped cilantro

Garnish

mint or cilantro sprigs

NUTRITION FACTS	
Amount per Serving	
Calories 105	Calories from Fat 9
	% Daily Value
Total Fat 1g	1.5%
Saturated Fat 0.2g	1%
Polyunsaturated Fat 0.5g	0%
Monounsaturated Fat 0.2g	0%
Cholesterol 0mg	0%
Sodium 203mg	8.5%
Total Carbohydrate 22g	7%
Dietary Fiber 3g	12%
Sugars 8.5g	0%
Protein 3g	0%

Percent daily values are based on a 2000 calorie diet

≈ Cut the beans into 2-inch lengths and place them in a saucepan of boiling water. Cook for 3 minutes, then add the corn and cook for another 3–4 minutes, or until tender but still crisp.

≈ Drain the vegetables well, season them to taste, and toss with coconut, mint, and cilantro. Arrange the vegetables in serving dishes, and garnish each one with a sprig of herb.

AVOCADO AND POMEGRANATE SALAD

SERVES 4

Avocados are popular and are used in many salads and appetizer dishes. Oranges and pomegranates combine perfectly in this salad which makes an unusual first course or side dish for a main meal.

≈ In a small bowl, whisk together wine vinegar, orange juice, salt and pepper to taste and honey. Slowly whisk in olive oil and vegetable oil until dressing is thick and creamy. Stir in the chopped mint. Set aside.

≈ Into a medium bowl, scrape seeds out of pomegranate halves. Add grape halves and toss to mix.

≈ Cut avocados in half and remove pits. Using a round-bladed knife, run it between skin and flesh of avocados, working skin away from flesh until skin is removed.

≈ Place avocados, round-side up, on work surface and, using a sharp knife and starting ½ inch below stem end, cut avocado lengthwise into ¼-inch slices, leaving stem end intact. Arrange each sliced avocado half on 4 individual plates. Using palm of hand, gently push avocado slices forward to fan out slices. Sprinkle lemon juice over them.

≈ Sprinkle a quarter of the pomegranate seed-grape mixture on to each avocado half and spoon over dressing. Garnish each plate with a few mint leaves.

1 ripe pomegranate, cut in half
1 cup black grapes, cut in half and seeded
2 small ripe avocados
1 tbsp lemon juice

Dressing
4 tbsp white-wine vinegar
2 tbsp orange juice
salt and freshly ground black pepper
1 tsp honey
1 tsp olive oil
1 tbsp peanut or sunflower oil
2 tbsp chopped fresh mint

Garnish
fresh mint leaves

NUTRITION FACTS	
Amount per Serving	
Calories 194	Calories from Fat 135
	% Daily Value
Total Fat 15g	23%
Saturated Fat 3g	15%
Polyunsaturated Fat 2g	0%
Monounsaturated Fat 9g	0%
Cholesterol 0mg	0%
Sodium 5mg	0.2%
Total Carbohydrate 13g	4%
Dietary Fiber 6g	24%
Sugars 12g	0%
Protein 2g	0%

Percent daily values are based on a 2000 calorie diet

LIMA BEAN AND MUSHROOM SOUP

SERVES 4

A traditional farmhouse dish, this soup is high in both fiber and nutrients; the lima beans are a very good source of zinc and potassium.

¼ lb lima beans, soaked overnight in cold water

1 tsp sunflower oil

2 medium onions, chopped

2 celery stalks, sliced

½ lb potatoes, peeled or scrubbed and diced

¼ lb button mushrooms, trimmed and sliced

¼ cup canned corn drained

1¼ cup skimmed milk

salt and freshly ground black pepper

Garnish

2 tbsp chopped parsley

NUTRITION FACTS	
Amount per Serving	
Calories 195	Calories from Fat 27
	% Daily Value
Total Fat 3g	5%
Saturated Fat 0.5g	2.5%
Polyunsaturated Fat 2g	0%
Monounsaturated Fat 0.5g	0%
Cholesterol 2mg	0.6%
Sodium 110mg	4.5%
Total Carbohydrate 34g	11%
Dietary Fiber 8g	32%
Sugars 9g	0%
Protein 10g	0%

Percent daily values are based on a 2000 calorie diet

≈ Drain the beans and place them in a large saucepan covered with fresh water. Boil them rapidly for 10 minutes, then simmer them for 35–40 minutes until they are soft. Drain the beans and reserve 1 pint of the stock.

≈ Heat the oil in a large saucepan, and fry the onion over medium heat until it softens. Add the celery and potato, and cook for 2–3 minutes, stirring.

≈ Add the reserved stock and mushrooms, bring to a boil, then cover and simmer for 10 minutes. Add the beans, corn, and milk, bring just to simmering point, and simmer for 2–3 minutes. Season to taste.

≈ Serve the soup in individual bowls, sprinkled with parsley.

ONION, LENTIL, AND LEMON SOUP

SERVES 6

*B*arley and lentils are two Armenian favorites paired in this earthy soup. Served
with warm cornbread, it would make a filling supper or lunch.

1 cup water

⅓ cup plus 1 tbsp pearl barley

1 tbsp tomato paste

6¼ cups vegetable stock

¾ cup lentils, rinsed and picked over

5 onions, sliced very thinly

1 tsp dried anise seeds

juice of 1 large lemon

large pinch of sweet paprika

pinch of cayenne pepper

salt and freshly ground black pepper

Garnish

12 paper-thin lemon slices

≈ Bring the water to a boil in a large
enameled or stainless steel saucepan. Stir
in the barley, cover, and simmer over low
heat for about 20–25 minutes, until the
barley is just tender and the water has
been absorbed. Stir in the tomato paste,
vegetable stock, lentils, onions, and
anise. Bring to a boil, cover, and simmer
over low heat for 1 hour, or until the
lentils are soft.

≈ Stir in the lemon juice, paprika,
cayenne pepper, and salt and pepper to
taste, and simmer uncovered for a
further 20 minutes. Pour the soup into
heated bowls, and garnish each with two
very thin slices of lemon.

NUTRITION FACTS	
Amount per Serving	
Calories 137	Calories from Fat 9
	% Daily Value
Total Fat 1g	1.5%
Saturated Fat 0.1g	0.5%
Polyunsaturated Fat 0.4g	0%
Monounsaturated Fat 0.1g	0%
Cholesterol 0mg	0%
Sodium 15mg	0.6%
Total Carbohydrate 27g	9%
Dietary Fiber 3g	12%
Sugars 3.5g	0%
Protein 7g	0%

Percent daily values are based on a 2000 calorie diet

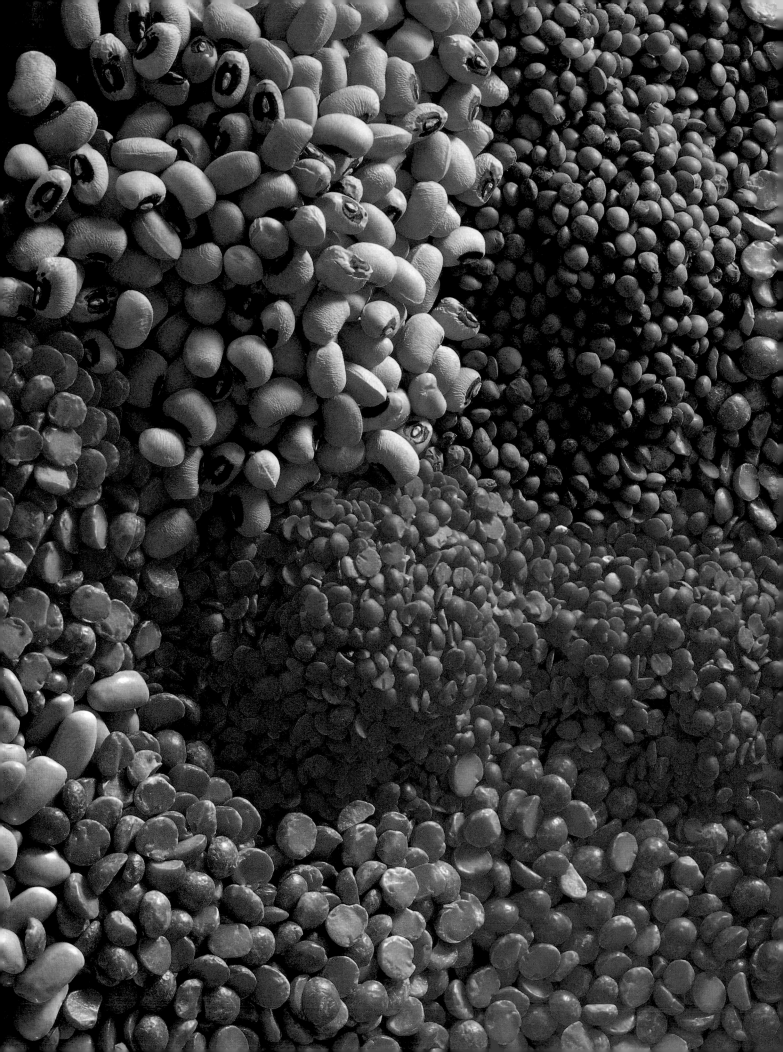

MAIN DISHES

Baked Mushroom Burgers

Baked Potatoes with Broccoli

Potatoes with Garbanzo Beans

Potato-topped Vegetable Pie

Spaghetti with Tomato and Basil Sauce

Mushroom and Broccoli Nut Loaf

Spiced Carrots and Corn with Bread Crumb Topping

Chinese Mustard Greens with Fusilli

Mushroom and Tomato Sauce

Spicy Mushroom Omelet

Creamed Celery Sauce

Cauliflower and Zucchini Sauce

Tunisian-style Vegetable Couscous

Peppers with Apricot and Hazelnut Filling

Zucchini Ragout

Five Vegetable Bhaji with Mint

Ginger and Garlic Egg and Pea Curry

Braised Okra with Chili Peppers

Potato and Tomato Pie

Eggplant with Spicy Potatoes and Tomato

Zucchini and Sweetcorn Crunch

Thai Noodles with Chili Peppers and Vegetables

Vegetable Medley

Armenian Vegetable Stew

BAKED MUSHROOM BURGERS

SERVES 4

These vegetable burgers freeze well, and can be cooked without thawing first. If frozen, add 5 minutes to the cooking time.

⅝ cup vegetable stock

2 medium onions, finely chopped

2 cloves garlic, crushed

½ lb mushrooms, trimmed and finely chopped

2 tbsp fine oatmeal

⅔ cup rolled oats

1 tbsp tomato paste

salt and freshly ground black pepper

2 tbsp chopped walnuts

2 tbsp chopped mint

Coating

a little skimmed milk

about ½ cup rolled oats

Garnish

1–2 tbsp chopped mint

tomato wedges (optional)

NUTRITION FACTS	
Amount per Serving	
Calories 177	Calories from Fat 60
	% Daily Value
Total Fat 6.5g	10%
Saturated Fat 0.7g	3.5%
Polyunsaturated Fat 3g	0%
Monounsaturated Fat 1g	0%
Cholesterol 0mg	0%
Sodium 22mg	9%
Total Carbohydrate 25g	8%
Dietary Fiber 5g	20%
Sugars 4g	0%
Protein 6g	0%

Percent daily values are based on a 2000 calorie diet

≈ Set the oven to 350°F. Put 6 tablespoons of the stock in a pan, add the onion and garlic, and bring to a boil. Simmer uncovered for 3–4 minutes, stirring once or twice. Stir in the mushrooms and cook for 3–4 minutes, then add the oatmeal and cook for 1 minute.

≈ Stir in the rolled oats and tomato paste and gradually pour on the remaining stock, stirring constantly. Season with salt and pepper, stir in the walnuts and mint, and remove from the heat. Add a little more stock or skimmed milk if the mixture is too thick; cook it over low heat for a minute or so if it is too runny. It should be a thick paste.

≈ Separate the mixture into 8 pieces, and shape each portion into patties. Dip each one first in milk and then in rolled oats to cover them evenly on all sides.

≈ Place the burgers on a non-stick cookie sheet, and bake them in the oven for 20–25 minutes, turning them once, until they are well browned. Garnish and serve while still hot.

BAKED POTATOES WITH BROCCOLI

SERVES 4

When you want to cook four large potatoes in a hurry, boiling them in their skins is quicker than cooking them in a microwave or in the oven.

≈ Cook the potatoes in boiling, salted water for 20–25 minutes, until they are soft. For a crisper skin, place the potatoes under hot heat for about 5 minutes. Meanwhile, cook the broccoli in boiling, salted water for 8–10 minutes, until it is just tender. Take care not to overcook it. Drain the potatoes and broccoli.

≈ Cut the potatoes in half, scoop out the pulp and mash it. Reserve 8 small florets of broccoli for garnish, and chop the rest. Mix the chopped broccoli, cheese, walnuts, and raisins with the potato, and season the mixture with salt and pepper.

≈ Spoon the filling into the potato skins and garnish each one with a broccoli floret. Serve hot.

4 large potatoes, scrubbed

salt

½ lb broccoli spears

¾ cup low-fat cottage cheese, strained

2 tbsp chopped walnuts

2 tbsp seedless raisins

freshly ground black pepper

NUTRITION FACTS	
Amount per Serving	
Calories 292	Calories from Fat 45
	% Daily Value
Total Fat 5g	8%
Saturated Fat 1g	5%
Polyunsaturated Fat 2g	0%
Monounsaturated Fat 1g	0%
Cholesterol 2mg	0.6%
Sodium 189mg	8%
Total Carbohydrate 51g	17%
Dietary Fiber 7g	28%
Sugars 14g	0%
Protein 14g	0%

Percent daily values are based on a 2000 calorie diet

POTATOES WITH GARBANZO BEANS

SERVES 6

This is another popular, filling dish, which can do service as a side dish if served without the fresh spinach that is stirred into the potatoes and garbanzo beans in the last 5 minutes of cooking.

⅓ cup olive oil

1 large onion, chopped

12 oz small red potatoes, washed and cut into small pieces

2 garlic cloves, finely chopped

2½ cups cooked and drained garbanzo beans

1 lb fresh spinach, chopped

5 medium tomatoes, peeled, seeded, and chopped

cayenne pepper

½ tsp coriander seeds

salt and freshly ground pepper

1 cup finely chopped fresh parsley

≈ Heat the olive oil in a flameproof casserole with a cover. Add the onion and cook until it is lightly colored and limp.

≈ Add the chopped potatoes and the garlic, and cook, stirring, over low heat for 3–4 minutes. Stir in the garbanzo beans, the tomatoes, cayenne pepper to taste, and the coriander seeds.

≈ Cover and simmer for 15–20 minutes, or until the potatoes are soft. Stir in the fresh spinach in the last 5 minutes of cooking and leave to wilt. Season to taste and stir in the chopped parsley before serving.

≈ This dish can also be cooled, chilled overnight, and served cold.

NUTRITION FACTS	
Amount per Serving	
Calories 245	Calories from Fat 144
	% Daily Value
Total Fat 16g	24%
Saturated Fat 2g	10%
Polyunsaturated Fat 2g	0%
Monounsaturated Fat 11g	0%
Cholesterol 0mg	0%
Sodium 120mg	5%
Total Carbohydrate 20g	7%
Dietary Fiber 4g	16%
Sugars 5g	0%
Protein 6g	0%

Percent daily values are based on a 2000 calorie diet

POTATO-TOPPED VEGETABLE PIE

SERVES 4

Cook the potatoes whole in their skins to retain maximum nutrients; once cooked they can easily be peeled and mashed. This dish can be prepared the previous day if necessary.

½ cup green lentils, washed and
    drained
3 cups barley, washed and drained
1 medium onion, chopped
14-oz can chopped tomatoes
2 cups cauliflower florets
2 celery stalks, sliced
1 leek, thickly sliced
1 turnip, thinly sliced
2 carrots, diced
2 tsp mixed dry herbs
1½ lb potatoes, scrubbed
3 tbsp low-fat milk
salt and freshly ground black pepper
⅓ cup low-fat medium-hard cheese,
    grated

≈ Set the oven to 400°F. Place the lentils, barley, onion, tomatoes (with juice), cauliflower, celery, leek, turnip, carrots, and herbs in a large saucepan and add 1¼ cups water. Bring to a boil, cover and simmer for 40–45 minutes or until the lentils, barley, and vegetables are just tender.

≈ Cook the potatoes in boiling, salted water for about 20 minutes, or until they are soft. Drain, peel, and mash them with the milk, and season to taste.

≈ Place the lentil mixture in a baking dish and pipe or fork the mashed potato on top to cover. Sprinkle the cheese on top, and bake the pie in the oven for 30–35 minutes, until it is evenly light brown. Serve hot. A tomato and herb salad makes a good accompaniment.

NUTRITION FACTS	
Amount per Serving	
Calories 355	Calories from Fat 27
	% Daily Value
Total Fat 3g	5%
Saturated Fat 1g	5%
Polyunsaturated Fat 1g	0%
Monounsaturated Fat 0.5g	0%
Cholesterol 4mg	1.3%
Sodium 142mg	6%
Total Carbohydrate 70g	23%
Dietary Fiber 10g	40%
Sugars 11g	0%
Protein 16g	0%

Percent daily values are based on a 2000 calorie diet

SPAGHETTI WITH TOMATO AND BASIL SAUCE

SERVES 4

Whole-wheat spaghetti has a mild, nutty flavor and a high fiber content. You can, if you wish, combine it with spinach pasta which derives its attractive color from its spinach content.

1 tbsp olive oil

1 medium onion, chopped

4 celery stalks, chopped

1 green chili pepper, seeded and finely chopped

2 cloves garlic, crushed

1½ lb tomatoes, skinned and roughly chopped

3 tbsp tomato paste

4 tbsp water

1 tbsp chopped basil

1 tsp chopped marjoram

¾ lb whole-wheat spaghetti

¼ cup black olives, stoned

¼ cup low-fat hard cheese, grated

¼ cup pine nuts

Garnish

basil sprigs

≈ Heat the oil in a saucepan, add the onion, celery, chili pepper, and garlic and fry over medium heat for about 3 minutes, until soft. Add the tomatoes and tomato paste, 4 tablespoons water, and half the chopped basil and marjoram. Bring to a boil and simmer for 10 minutes.

≈ Place the spaghetti in a large pan of boiling water, and cook for 12 minutes, or until just tender. (If you are using green spaghetti, add it to the pan 2 minutes after the whole-wheat spaghetti, and return the water to a boil.

≈ Drain the pasta into a colander, and refresh it by running hot water through it. Drain it thoroughly and divide it among four dinner plates.

≈ Stir the olives and remaining herbs into the sauce, and spoon on top of the spaghetti. Sprinkle with the cheese and pine nuts and garnish with basil sprigs.

NUTRITION FACTS	
Amount per Serving	
Calories 504	Calories from Fat 180
	% Daily Value
Total Fat 20g	31%
Saturated Fat 3g	15%
Polyunsaturated Fat 7g	0%
Monounsaturated Fat 8g	0%
Cholesterol 4mg	1%
Sodium 518mg	22%
Total Carbohydrate 67g	22%
Dietary Fiber 15g	60%
Sugars 12g	0%
Protein 19g	0%

Percent daily values are based on a 2000 calorie diet

MUSHROOM AND BROCCOLI NUT LOAF

SERVES 4

With its colorful layer of broccoli spears, this vegetarian loaf is both attractive and appetizing. It is equally good served hot or cold, and freezes well.

≈ Set the oven to 350°F. Sauté the mushrooms in a skillet with half of the margarine. Drain the slices, and place them in a line down the center of a lightly greased 7½ x 5 x 3 inch loaf pan.

≈ Cook the celery, garlic, and onion in the same skillet until softened. Stir in the flour and tomatoes (with juice), and cook until the mixture thickens. Add the bread crumbs, nuts, egg, herbs, and seasoning, and remove from the heat. Spread half of the mixture in the loaf pan. Add the broccoli spears, and top with the remaining mixture.

≈ Cover the pan with foil, place it in a roasting pan half-filled with boiling water, and bake in the oven for 1¼–1½ hours.

≈ For the sauce, melt the remaining margarine, add the chopped mushrooms, and cook for 2–3 minutes. Stir in the flour, and cook for 1 minute. Add the stock, milk, and seasoning and stir for 1–2 minutes, until thickened.

≈ Turn out the loaf on to a heated serving dish, and serve the sauce separately. Garnish the dish with celery leaves.

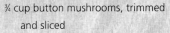

¾ cup button mushrooms, trimmed and sliced

⅛ cup polyunsaturated margarine

2 celery stalks, sliced

1 clove garlic, crushed

1 medium onion, grated

1 tbsp whole-wheat flour

14-oz can chopped tomatoes

2 cups whole-wheat bread crumbs

½ cup ground walnuts

1 egg

1 tsp chopped basil

1 tsp chopped oregano

1 tbsp chopped parsley

salt and freshly ground black pepper

¼ lb broccoli spears, cooked

Sauce

⅛ lb mushrooms, trimmed and chopped

1 tbsp whole-wheat flour

½ cup vegetable stock

½ cup skimmed milk

Garnish

celery leaves

NUTRITION FACTS		
Amount per Serving		
Calories 269	Calories from Fat 144	
		% Daily Value
Total Fat 16g		24%
Saturated Fat 2g		10%
Polyunsaturated Fat 9g		0%
Monounsaturated Fat 4g		0%
Cholesterol 60mg		20%
Sodium 281mg		12%
Total Carbohydrate 21g		7%
Dietary Fiber 7g		24%
Sugars 6g		0%
Protein 10g		0%

Percent daily values are based on a 2000 calorie diet

SPICED CARROTS AND CORN WITH BREAD CRUMB TOPPING

SERVES 4

An unusual blend of vegetables and spices with a crunchy topping, this is a dish to make now and cook later.

1 lb carrots, scraped and thinly sliced

salt

7-oz can corn

1 tbsp clear honey

½ tsp ground ginger

large pinch grated nutmeg

3 tbsp vegetable stock

2 tbsp chopped mint

pepper

oil, for brushing

Topping

4 tbsp whole-wheat bread crumbs

1 tbsp sesame seeds

1 tbsp sunflower seeds

¼ cup whole-wheat flour

5 tbsp sunflower oil

salt and freshly ground black pepper

NUTRITION FACTS

Amount per Serving (ie 1 tbsp)	
Calories 311	Calories from Fat 170

	% Daily Value
Total Fat 19g	29%
Saturated Fat 2g	10%
Polyunsaturated Fat 11g	0%
Monounsaturated Fat 4g	0%
Cholesterol 0mg	0%
Sodium 202mg	8%
Total Carbohydrate 33g	11%
Dietary Fiber 6g	24%
Sugars 17g	0%
Protein 5g	0%

Percent daily values are based on a 2000 calorie diet

≈ Set the oven to 375°F. Steam the carrots over boiling, salted water for 8–10 minutes, until they are just tender. Mix them with the corn, honey, ginger, nutmeg, stock, and mint, and season with salt and pepper.

≈ Lightly brush a 2-pint ovenproof dish with oil. Spoon in the vegetable mixture, and level the top.

≈ Mix together the bread crumbs, seeds, and flour, and gradually pour on the oil, stirring. Season the mixture with salt and pepper, and spread it over the vegetable layer. Bake the dish in the oven for 20 minutes until the topping is golden brown. Serve hot.

CHINESE MUSTARD GREENS WITH FUSILLI

SERVES 4

This quick-to-prepare, nutritious dish is perfect for a light lunch when entertaining friends.

3½ cups dried fusilli (small twists)

dash of olive oil

3 tbsp sesame oil

3 cloves of garlic, crushed

2 carrots, peeled and cut into ribbons

8 scallions, stalks removed and leaves shredded

5–6 tbsp dark soy sauce

3 tbsp toasted sesame seeds

≈ Bring a large saucepan of water to a boil, and add the fusilli with a dash of olive oil. Cook for about 10 minutes, stirring occasionally, until the pasta is tender. Drain thoroughly, and set aside.

≈ To cut the carrots into wafer-thin ribbons, peel away the outside skin using a vegetable peeler, then continue peeling the carrot.

≈ Heat the sesame oil in a wok or large skillet, and add the garlic. Stir-fry for 30 seconds, then add the carrot ribbons. Continue to cook for 3–4 minutes, then add the shredded scallions. Cook for 2–3 minutes, stirring continuously.

≈ Stir in the soy sauce, sesame seeds, and the fusilli. Cook for a further 2 minutes, and serve immediately.

49

NUTRITION FACTS	
Amount per Serving (2½ cups)	
Calories 465	Calories from Fat 153
	% Daily Value
Total Fat 17g	26%
Saturated Fat 2g	10%
Polyunsaturated Fat 7g	0%
Monounsaturated Fat 7g	0%
Cholesterol 0mg	0%
Sodium 17mg	0.7%
Total Carbohydrate 70g	23%
Dietary Fiber 6.5g	26%
Sugars 7g	0%
Protein 13g	0%

Percent daily values are based on a 2000 calorie diet

MUSHROOM AND TOMATO SAUCE

SERVES 4

Ladle this quick and easy sauce over piping hot pasta and offer freshly grated low-fat cheese to sprinkle on top.

4 tbsp olive oil

2 garlic cloves, crushed

1 lb mushrooms, sliced

1 bunch scallions, chopped

salt and freshly ground black pepper

1 bay leaf

2 × 14 oz cans chopped tomatoes

2 tbsp tomato paste

handful fresh basil sprigs, stalks
  discarded and leaves shredded

≈ Heat the oil in a large skillet or heavy-based saucepan. Add the garlic, mushrooms, scallions, seasoning, and bay leaf. Cook, stirring often, over medium heat for about 20 minutes, or until the mushrooms are well cooked and much of the liquor they yield has evaporated.

≈ Add the canned tomatoes and stir in the tomato paste, then bring to a boil and reduce the heat. Simmer for 3 minutes, then taste for seasoning. Stir in the basil and serve the sauce.

NUTRITION FACTS

Amount per Serving

Calories 160	Calories from Fat 108
	% Daily Value
Total Fat 12g	18%
Saturated Fat 2g	10%
Polyunsaturated Fat 1g	0%
Monounsaturated Fat 8g	0%
Cholesterol 0mg	0%
Sodium 104mg	4%
Total Carbohydrate 9g	3%
Dietary Fiber 4.5g	18%
Sugars 8g	0%
Protein 5g	0%

Percent daily values are based on a 2000 calorie diet

SPICY MUSHROOM OMELET

SERVES 2

≈ Separate the eggs, keeping the whites and yolks in separate bowls and beating each.

≈ Fold the flour into the egg yolks, together with the bell pepper, mushrooms, green chili pepper, onion, and all the herbs and spices.

≈ Mix the egg whites into the egg yolk mixture and beat once again, gradually adding 2 tablespoons of water.

≈ Grease a large, non-stick skillet with the oil and heat it to smoking point.

≈ Straight away, pour in the egg and vegetable mixture, reduce the heat and cook for 1 minute or so, shaking the pan. Then remove the pan to a hot broiler to finish cooking the omelet.

3 large eggs

1 tsp all-purpose flour

2 tbsp chopped green or red bell pepper

1 cup chopped button mushrooms

1 green chili pepper, finely chopped

⅓ cup thinly sliced onion

½ tsp chili powder

¼ tsp garlic powder

1–2 tbsp chopped cilantro leaves

¼ tsp cumin seeds

¼ tsp salt

1 tbsp oil

NUTRITION FACTS	
Amount per Serving	
Calories 235	Calories from Fat 144

	% Daily Value
Total Fat 16g	25%
Saturated Fat 3g	15%
Polyunsaturated Fat 5g	0%
Monounsaturated Fat 6g	0%
Cholesterol 357mg	119%
Sodium 133mg	5.5%
Total Carbohydrate 11g	4%
Dietary Fiber 2g	8%
Sugars 2.5g	0%
Protein 14g	0%

Percent daily values are based on a 2000 calorie diet

CREAMED CELERY
SAUCE

SERVES 4

A creamy, low-fat sauce for serving with pasta – either as a topping for spaghetti or tagliatelle, or to layer with lasagne.

1 head celery

2 tbsp olive oil

1 onion, chopped

1 garlic clove, crushed (optional)

1 carrot, diced

1 bay leaf

3 tbsp all-purpose flour

8 fl oz dry white wine

8 fl oz vegetable stock

salt and freshly ground black pepper

4 oz low-fat soft cheese

1–2 tbsp chopped fresh tarragon or a
handful of basil sprigs, trimmed
and shredded (optional)

NUTRITION FACTS	
Amount per Serving	
Calories 194	Calories from Fat 80
	% Daily Value
Total Fat 9g	14%
Saturated Fat 2.5g	12.5%
Polyunsaturated Fat 0.75g	0%
Monounsaturated Fat 5g	0%
Cholesterol 8mg	3%
Sodium 54mg	2%
Total Carbohydrate 16g	5%
Dietary Fiber 3g	12%
Sugars 4g	0%
Protein 4g	0%

Percent daily values are based on a 2000 calorie diet

≈ Trim the celery, discarding the root end and tips of the stalks. Reserve the leafy part and chop it fine (since it can be added to the sauce). Separate the stalks, scrub them, then dice each one. This is not difficult – cut them lengthways into 3 or 4 strips, then across into dice.

≈ Heat the oil in a large, heavy-based saucepan. Add the onion, garlic (if used), carrot, bay leaf, and celery (chopped stalks and leaves). Stir well over medium heat for 5 minutes, then cover the pan and cook gently for 15 minutes to soften the vegetables.

≈ Stir in the flour, then gradually pour in the wine and stock. Bring to a boil, reduce the heat and simmer gently, uncovered, for 20 minutes, stirring occasionally. Add seasoning to taste and stir in the low-fat cheese. Do not boil. Remove from the heat and add the tarragon or basil, then serve at once.

CAULIFLOWER AND ZUCCHINI SAUCE

SERVES 4

This is a tomato-based sauce to serve with spaghetti, fettuccine, tagliatelle, long macaroni, pappardelle, or mafaldine – in other words, long types of pasta.

2 tbsp olive oil

1 large onion, chopped

1 bay leaf

1 garlic clove, crushed

6 oz cauliflower, divided into small florets

2 tbsp chopped fresh oregano

2 cups tomato paste

⅔ cup water

salt and freshly ground black pepper

1 lb zucchini, sliced

10 black olives, pitted and thickly sliced (optional)

freshly grated low-fat cheese, to serve

≈ Heat the oil in a large saucepan. Add the onion, bay leaf and garlic, then stir well, and cover the pan. Cook for 5 minutes.

≈ Add the cauliflower and oregano, stir well, and cover the pan again. Let cook for 5 minutes. Stir in the tomato paste, water and salt and pepper to taste. Bring to a boil, reduce the heat, and cover the pan. Simmer for 15 minutes.

≈ Finally, add the zucchini and olives, if using. Cover and continue to simmer gently for 10 minutes. Taste for seasoning before serving the sauce. The sauce and pasta can take generous quantities of low-fat cheese as a topping, but it is best to leave individual diner's options open.

NUTRITION FACTS	
Amount per Serving	
Calories 134	Calories from Fat 72
	% Daily Value
Total Fat 8g	12%
Saturated Fat 2g	10%
Polyunsaturated Fat 1g	0%
Monounsaturated Fat 5g	0%
Cholesterol 2mg	0.6%
Sodium 214mg	10%
Total Carbohydrate 8g	3%
Dietary Fiber 4g	16%
Sugars 7g	0%
Protein 7g	0%

Percent daily values are based on a 2000 calorie diet

TUNISIAN-STYLE VEGETABLE COUSCOUS

SERVES 4

A prominent feature of North African cooking, couscous is made from particles of hard durum wheat semolina. To pre-cook couscous grains, wash them thoroughly and steam uncovered over a bowl of fast-boiling water for 30 minutes. Spread the couscous on a plate, and sprinkle with cold water before continuing to cook it in this Tunisian-style recipe.

½ cup garbanzo beans, soaked overnight and drained

½ cup adzuki beans, soaked overnight and drained

2 cloves garlic, crushed

2 leeks, sliced

2 carrots, thinly sliced

2½ cups cauliflower florets

3 zucchini, sliced

1 parsnip, thinly sliced

2 tbsp tomato paste

2 tsp ground coriander

½ tsp ground turmeric

1 tsp mixed dry herbs

1¼ cups water

1 green bell pepper, seeded, cored, and sliced

¾ lb tomatoes, skinned and quartered

4 oz dry grains (to yield 8 oz precooked couscous); (see above)

2 tbsp low-fat yogurt

salt and paprika pepper

Garnish

fresh parsley

NUTRITION FACTS	
Amount per Serving	
Calories 328	Calories from Fat 27
	% Daily Value
Total Fat 3g	5%
Saturated Fat 0.5g	2.5%
Polyunsaturated Fat 1.5g	0%
Monounsaturated Fat 0.5g	0%
Cholesterol 0mg	0%
Sodium 51mg	2%
Total Carbohydrate 62g	21%
Dietary Fiber 11g	44%
Sugars 12g	0%
Protein 17g	0%

Percent daily values are based on a 2000 calorie diet

≈ Place the drained garbanzo beans and adzuki beans in separate saucepans, cover with water, and boil rapidly for 10 minutes. Cover and simmer for 30–40 minutes.

≈ Place the garlic, leeks, carrots, cauliflower, zucchini, parsnip, tomato paste, coriander, turmeric, and herbs in a large saucepan. Add water, bring to a boil, then cover and simmer for 20 minutes.

≈ Add the garbanzo beans, adzuki beans, green bell pepper, and tomatoes to the vegetables. Return to a boil.

≈ Place the partly-cooked couscous in a steamer lined with a double thickness of cheesecloth, or a clean dishtowel and place over the pan of vegetables. Cover and cook for 15 minutes, stirring the grains once or twice.

≈ Stir the low-fat yogurt into the couscous, and put in a heated serving dish. Season and garnish the vegetables and serve them in another heated dish.

PEPPERS WITH APRICOT AND HAZELNUT FILLING

SERVES 4

This is a good main dish to offer a vegetarian guest. The colorful peppers have visual appeal, and the apricot and hazelnut filling provides fiber, protein, and vitamins.

≈ Set the oven to 375°F. Place the bulgur wheat in a bowl, pour over 1¼ cup boiling water, and leave to stand for about 15 minutes.

≈ Place the bell peppers in a shallow, lightly oiled dish. Heat 1 tablespoon oil in a saucepan, and fry the onion over medium heat for about 3 minutes, until it is soft. Stir in the bulgur wheat, hazelnuts, apricots, ginger, and cardamom. Cook for 1 minute longer, stirring continuously. Add the cilantro and yogurt, mix well, and remove from the heat.

≈ Pile the filling into the pepper shells. Cover the dish with foil and bake in the oven for 30–35 minutes. Garnish with cilantro leaves to serve.

1 cup bulgur wheat

2 red bell peppers, cut in half lengthwise, seeded, and cored

2 yellow bell peppers, cut in half lengthwise, seeded, and cored

1 tbsp sunflower oil, plus extra for brushing

1 medium onion, chopped

⅓ cup hazelnuts, chopped

½ cup dried apricots, chopped

½ tsp ground ginger

1 tsp ground cardamom

2 tbsp chopped cilantro

3 tbsp plain low-fat yogurt

Garnish

cilantro leaves

NUTRITION FACTS	
Amount per Serving	
Calories 353	Calories from Fat 90
	% Daily Value
Total Fat 10g	15%
Saturated Fat 1g	5%
Polyunsaturated Fat 2.5g	0%
Monounsaturated Fat 5g	0%
Cholesterol 1mg	0.3%
Sodium 50mg	2%
Total Carbohydrate 59g	20%
Dietary Fiber 9g	36%
Sugars 30g	0%
Protein 10g	0%

Percent daily values are based on a 2000 calorie diet

ZUCCHINI RAGOUT

SERVES 4

This is a good way of turning zucchini into a delicious supper dish or vegetarian meal. Making your own bouquet garni is important — it is better to change the herbs according to availability than to compromise with a ready-made selection.

3 tbsp olive oil

2 onions, chopped

4 celery sticks, chopped

2 carrots, diced

2 garlic cloves, crushed

1 bouquet garni

4 tbsp tomato paste

14-oz can chopped tomatoes

salt and freshly ground black pepper

1½ lb zucchini, peeled, seeded and thickly sliced

3 oz fresh whole-wheat bread crumbs

2 tbsp chopped parsley

3 oz low-fat hard cheese, grated

≈ Heat the oil in a flameproof casserole. Add the onions, celery, carrots, garlic, and bouquet garni. Stir well until sizzling, then cover and cook over medium heat for 20 minutes, stirring once.

≈ Stir in the tomato paste and canned tomatoes with plenty of seasoning. Bring to a boil. Add the zucchini and mix well. Reduce the heat so that the mixture barely simmers, cover and cook very gently for 1 hour, stirring occasionally. The zucchini should be tender but not mushy.

≈ Set the oven at 400°F.

≈ Mix the bread crumbs, cheese and parsley, then sprinkle the mixture over the zucchini. Bake for 20–30 minutes, until crisp and golden on top, then serve at once. If preferred, the topping may be cooked under a broiler heated to a medium setting, until crisp and golden-brown.

NUTRITION FACTS	
Amount per Serving	
Calories 232	Calories from Fat 108
	% Daily Value
Total Fat 12g	18%
Saturated Fat 3g	15%
Polyunsaturated Fat 1g	0%
Monounsaturated Fat 7g	0%
Cholesterol 8mg	3%
Sodium 320mg	13%
Total Carbohydrate 21g	7%
Dietary Fiber 6g	24%
Sugars 12g	0%
Protein 11g	0%

Percent daily values are based on a 2000 calorie diet

FIVE VEGETABLE BHAJI WITH MINT

SERVES 4

Traditionally Indian, a bhaji is a spiced vegetable dish. This one is fun because every time it is cooked it has a new taste — as the combination of the five vegetables is somehow never quite the same.

¼ lb green beans

6 oz potatoes

¼ lb carrots

6 oz eggplant

¼ lb tomatoes

1–2 green chili peppers

2 tbsp oil

7–8 cloves garlic, finely chopped

½ tsp chili powder

¼ tsp ground turmeric

½–¾ tsp salt

2–3 tbsp mint or cilantro leaves

NUTRITION FACTS	
Amount per Serving	
Calories 113	Calories from Fat 54
	% Daily Value
Total Fat 6g	9%
Saturated Fat 1g	5%
Polyunsaturated Fat 4g	0%
Monounsaturated Fat 1g	0%
Cholesterol 0mg	0%
Sodium 13mg	0.5%
Total Carbohydrate 13g	0.5%
Dietary Fiber 4g	16%
Sugars 4g	0%
Protein 3g	0%

Percent daily values are based on a 2000 calorie diet

≈ Top and tail and string the beans, then chop them into bite-size pieces.

≈ Cut the potatoes into quarters and halve them again, preferably leaving the skin on.

≈ Scrape and dice the carrots.

≈ Cut the eggplant into four strips lengthwise and then slice across into ½-inch chunks.

≈ Roughly chop the tomatoes and green chilies.

≈ Measure the oil into a medium-sized heavy-bottomed saucepan over a medium heat. Add the garlic, stirring it as soon as it begins to turn translucent, then add all the vegetables. Also stir in the chili powder, turmeric, and salt. Mix the spices together thoroughly.

≈ Lower the heat, cover the pan and cook for another 20–25 minutes.

≈ Add the mint or cilantro leaves, stir and switch the heat off. Let it stand for 2–3 minutes before serving.

GINGER AND GARLIC EGG AND PEA CURRY

SERVES 4

4 large eggs

2 tbsp oil

⅓ cup chopped onion

¼ tsp cumin seeds

2 tsp ginger and garlic paste (from Asian stores)

½ tsp chili powder

¼ tsp turmeric

½ tsp ground coriander

salt to taste

¼ tsp garam masala (available from Asian stores)

⅓ cup chopped tomato

scant 1 cup fresh or frozen peas

1 green chili pepper, slit

2 tbsp cilantro leaves

≈ Hard-boil the eggs, remove their shells, then set aside.

≈ Heat the oil in a medium-sized heavy-bottomed saucepan and fry the onion and cumin seeds until the onion is light gold in color.

≈ Add the ginger and garlic paste, chili powder, turmeric, ground coriander, salt, and garam masala and fry this mixture well for a couple of minutes, adding, whenever needed, 1 tablespoon of water, to prevent burning or sticking.

≈ Add the whole eggs and tomato, stir gently and cook for a minute.

≈ Add 1¼ cups of water and let it come to a boil before adding the peas and green chili. Cook for another 5 minutes.

≈ Stir in the cilantro leaves and remove the pan from the heat.

NUTRITION FACTS	
Amount per Serving	
Calories 150	Calories from Fat 108
	% Daily Value
Total Fat 12g	18%
Saturated Fat 2.5g	12.5%
Polyunsaturated Fat 4g	0%
Monounsaturated Fat 4g	0%
Cholesterol 238mg	79%
Sodium 90mg	3%
Total Carbohydrate 3g	1%
Dietary Fiber 1g	4%
Sugars 2g	0%
Protein 8g	0%

Percent daily values are based on a 2000 calorie diet

OKRA WITH CHILI PEPPERS

SERVES 4

1 lb okra

2 tbsp sunflower oil

1 large onion, thinly sliced

4 green chili peppers, seeded and
  sliced

1 green bell pepper, seeded and
  sliced

6 oz tomatoes, peeled, seeded and
  chopped

salt and freshly ground black pepper

3 tbsp water

plain yogurt, to serve

NUTRITION FACTS	
Amount per Serving	
Calories 128	Calories from Fat 63
	% Daily Value
Total Fat 7g	11%
Saturated Fat 1g	5%
Polyunsaturated Fat 4g	0%
Monounsaturated Fat 1.5g	0%
Cholesterol 2mg	0.6%
Sodium 47mg	2%
Total Carbohydrate 10g	3%
Dietary Fiber 8g	32%
Sugars 9g	0%
Protein 6g	0%

Percent daily values are based on a 2000 calorie diet

≈ Trim the okra and prick a few times with a fork.

≈ Heat the oil in a pan and sauté the onion and chili peppers for 5 minutes, or until softened. Add the green bell pepper and cook for a further 2 minutes.

≈ Stir in the chopped tomatoes, the okra and water with seasoning to taste and bring to a boil. Reduce the heat, cover the pan and simmer for 8 minutes, or until the okra is tender. Serve immediately topped with yogurt.

POTATO AND TOMATO PIE

SERVES 4

T wo favorite vegetables are brought together in this simple yet tasty recipe from Portugal. It makes a good supper or lunch dish, or a vegetarian main course, and is a useful way of using leftover cooked potatoes.

≈ To make the red bell pepper paste stir together the bell peppers and salt; then leave, uncovered, at room temperature for 24 hours.

≈ Preheat the broiler. Rinse the bell peppers well, drain and pat dry. Place, skin side up, on a baking sheet. Broil until the skins are charred and blistered. Leave to cool slightly before peeling off the skins and discarding.

≈ Purée the garlic and bell peppers in a blender, pouring in the oil slowly.

≈ Preheat the oven to 400°F.

≈ Lay the potato slices in a well-oiled, shallow baking dish. Spread thinly with red bell pepper paste.

≈ Chop the parsley, garlic, and chili pepper together and mix with the oil. Add lemon juice and seasoning to taste and spread half over the potatoes.

≈ Cover with the tomatoes and spoon over the remaining parsley mixture. Trickle a little oil over the vegetables and bake for 30–40 minutes. Serve warm, not straight from the oven.

about 6 boiled or steamed medium-sized potatoes, thinly sliced

Red Bell Pepper Paste (see below), for spreading

1 bunch of parsley

1 garlic clove

1 fresh red chili pepper, seeded

3 tbsp virgin oil, plus extra for trickling

squeeze of lemon juice

salt and pepper

1¼ lb well-flavored tomatoes, skinned, seeded, and sliced

Red Bell Pepper Paste

3 large red bell peppers, seeded and quartered lengthwise

1 tbsp sea salt

2 garlic cloves

2 tbsp olive oil

NUTRITION FACTS	
Amount per Serving	
Calories 236	Calories from Fat 135
	% Daily Value
Total Fat 15g	23%
Saturated Fat 2g	10%
Polyunsaturated Fat 2g	0%
Monounsaturated Fat 10g	0%
Cholesterol 0mg	0%
Sodium 22mg	1%
Total Carbohydrate 24g	8%
Dietary Fiber 6g	24%
Sugars 13g	0%
Protein 4g	0%

Percent daily values are based on a 2000 calorie diet

EGGPLANT WITH SPICY POTATOES

SERVES 4

¾ lb eggplant

½ lb potatoes

2 tbsp oil

⅓ cup sliced onion

½ tsp cumin seeds

½ tsp roasted and crushed coriander
    seeds

½ tsp curry powder (optional)

1 tsp grated ginger root

4–5 cloves garlic, finely chopped

½ tsp chili powder

¼ tsp turmeric

salt to taste

1 tbsp low-fat plain yogurt

½ tsp sugar

1–2 green chili peppers, chopped

⅓ cup chopped tomato

1 tbsp lemon juice

2 tbsp chopped cilantro leaves

≈ Wash the eggplant. Cut it into quarters lengthwise, then, holding the pieces together, cut them across into ½-inch chunks.

≈ Scrub the potatoes thoroughly and do not peel them, then cut each one into quarters and each quarter twice or more so that you have at least twelve bite-sized pieces from each potato.

≈ Heat the oil in a medium-sized heavy-bottomed saucepan and fry the onion until it turns light brown.

≈ Add the cumin and coriander seeds and the curry leaves, if using. Fry these for a minute or so, then add the ginger, half the garlic, the chili powder, turmeric, and salt. Cook this mixture over quite a high heat, adding 2 tablespoons of water as necessary so that the spice paste deepens in color and does not stick. This should not take longer than 2 minutes.

≈ Add the eggplant, then the yogurt, sugar, and green chili peppers. Mix everything together and cook for 2 to 3 minutes. Add ⅔ cup of water, lower the heat and simmer for 15 minutes, with the lid firmly on.

≈ Add the potato, chili peppers, and tomato. Ensuring that the lid is firmly on, simmer for another 10 minutes, checking it occasionally to make sure that it is not sticking or burning. If it seems a bit too dry or you would prefer a little more sauce, just add a little more water and let it simmer for a few more minutes.

≈ Lastly, add the remaining garlic, the lemon juice, and cilantro leaves. Cook for 1 more minute, gently stir to mix it thoroughly, then turn off the heat.

NUTRITION FACTS

Amount per Serving

Calories 125	Calories from Fat 54
	% Daily Value
Total Fat 6g	9%
Saturated Fat 1g	5%
Polyunsaturated Fat 4g	0%
Monounsaturated Fat 1g	0%
Cholesterol 0mg	0%
Sodium 15mg	0.6%
Total Carbohydrate 15.5g	5%
Dietary Fiber 4g	16%
Sugars 5g	0%
Protein 3g	0%

Percent daily values are based on a 2000 calorie diet

ZUCCHINI AND SWEETCORN CRUNCH

SERVES 4

Semolina and cheese topping adds a pleasing crunch to this dish.

1½ lb zucchini, peeled, seeded, and
  thickly sliced

1 small onion, finely chopped

1 tsp ground mace

salt and freshly ground black pepper

1 bouquet garni

2 tsp olive oil

12-oz can corn, drained

2 oz walnuts, chopped

2 tbsp semolina

3 tbsp grated low-fat hard cheese

4 tbsp dry white bread crumbs

NUTRITION FACTS	
Amount per Serving	
Calories 219	Calories from Fat 108
	% Daily Value
Total Fat 12g	18%
Saturated Fat 2g	10%
Polyunsaturated Fat 6g	0%
Monounsaturated Fat 3g	0%
Cholesterol 3mg	0.1%
Sodium 1080mg	45%
Total Carbohydrate 19g	16%
Dietary Fiber 5g	20%
Sugars 6g	0%
Protein 9g	0%

Percent daily values are based on a 2000 calorie diet

≈ Place the zucchini, onion, and seasoning in a large flameproof casserole and mix well. Add the bouquet garni and the oil and mix again to coat the vegetables. Heat until the mixture begins to sizzle, then put a tight-fitting lid on the pan and cook gently for 25 minutes. Regulate the heat so that the mixture just murmurs in the pan.

≈ Add the corn, mix well and cook for 5 minutes, covered. The zucchini should be tender but firm.

≈ Mix the nuts, semolina, low-fat cheese, and bread crumbs, then sprinkle the mixture over the vegetables and put under a moderately hot broiler until evenly browned. If the mixture is browned too quickly it will become dark or burn, a lower heat is more successful. Serve straight away.

THAI NOODLES WITH CHILI PEPPERS AND VEGETABLES

SERVES 4

Rice or noodles, whether boiled or fried, form the basis of most meals in Thailand. Thai cooking is often slightly perfumed by the lemon grass which features strongly in many dishes.

6 oz thin vermicelli

1 tbsp sunflower oil

2 lemon grass stalks, outer leaves removed and chopped

1-inch piece root ginger, peeled and grated

1 red onion, cut into thin wedges

2 garlic cloves, crushed

4 red Thai chili peppers, seeded and sliced

1 red bell pepper, seeded and cut into matchsticks

4 oz carrot, very thinly sliced with a vegetable peeler

4 oz zucchini, trimmed and sliced with a vegetable peeler

3 oz snow peas, trimmed and cut diagonally in half

6 scallions, trimmed and diagonally sliced

2 oz cashew nuts

2 tbsp soy sauce

juice of 1 orange

1 tsp clear honey

1 tbsp sesame oil

≈ Cook the noodles in lightly salted boiling water for 3 minutes. Drain, plunge into cold water, then drain again and reserve.

≈ Heat the oil in a wok or large pan and stir-fry the lemon grass and ginger for 2 minutes. Discard the lemon grass and ginger, keeping the oil in the pan.

≈ Add the onion, garlic and chili peppers, and stir-fry for 2 minutes. Add the red bell pepper and cook for a further 2 minutes. Add the remaining vegetables and stir-fry for 2 minutes. Then add the reserved noodles and cashew nuts with the soy sauce, orange juice, and honey. Stir-fry for 1 minute. Add the sesame oil and stir-fry for 30 seconds. Serve immediately.

NUTRITION FACTS	
Amount per Serving	
Calories 342	Calories from Fat 135

	% Daily Value
Total Fat 15g	23%
Saturated Fat 2g	10%
Polyunsaturated Fat 4g	0%
Monounsaturated Fat 5g	0%
Cholesterol 0mg	0%
Sodium 192mg	8%
Total Carbohydrate 45g	15%
Dietary Fiber 5g	20%
Sugars 10g	0%
Protein 10g	0%

Percent daily values are based on a 2000 calorie diet

VEGETABLE MEDLEY

SERVES 4

This is a delicious sauce. Serve the mixed vegetables with shells, spirals, or pasta shapes rather than with long, thin pasta.

6 oz cauliflower, broken into small
    florets

salt and freshly ground black pepper

2 tbsp olive oil

2 tbsp butter

1 onion, chopped

6 oz baby carrots, quartered
    lengthways and thinly sliced

8 oz young zucchini, very lightly
    peeled and thinly sliced

1⅓ cups sliced button mushrooms

1 large, leafy sprig of tarragon,
    chopped

grated rind of ½ a lemon

squeeze of lemon juice

NUTRITION FACTS

Amount per Serving

Calories 134	Calories from Fat 100

	% Daily Value
Total Fat 11g	**17%**
Saturated Fat 4g	20%
Polyunsaturated Fat 1g	0%
Monounsaturated Fat 5g	0%
Cholesterol 12mg	**4%**
Sodium 62mg	**2.5%**
Total Carbohydrate 6g	**2%**
Dietary Fiber 4g	16%
Sugars 5g	0%
Protein 4g	**0%**

Percent daily values are based on a 2000 calorie diet

≈ Cook the cauliflower in boiling salted water for about 3 minutes, until lightly cooked. Drain well.

≈ Heat the olive oil and butter in a large saucepan. Add the onion, carrots, and cauliflower, and stir well; then cover the pan, and cook for 10 minutes. Shake the pan occasionally to prevent the vegetables sticking.

≈ Add the zucchini, mushrooms, tarragon, lemon rind and juice. Stir well, cover the pan again, and cook for a further 2–3 minutes, or until the zucchini are bright green and tender, but with a bit of bite and full of flavor. Taste for seasoning before serving.

ARMENIAN VEGETABLE STEW

SERVES 4

There are no hard and fast rules to making this Armenian specialty. It can incorporate whatever is in the refrigerator, for example, substitute turnip for carrots, cabbage for celery. It can be served as a main course or as a side dish.

≈ Preheat the oven to 350°F. Place the oil in a large enameled or stainless steel casserole and warm it over medium heat. Add the garlic and stir to flavor the oil, about 2 minutes. Pour in the stock and add the bay leaf, herbs, and seasoning to taste. Bring to a boil.

- ≈ Add the vegetables, little by little,
- stirring to combine as you add them.
- Cover the casserole with a lid or foil, and
- transfer to the oven. Bake for about 1
- hour or until the vegetables are all
- tender, stirring occasionally.

¼ cup plus 1 tbsp olive oil

4 cloves garlic, crushed

1 cup vegetable stock

1 bay leaf

½ tsp dried tarragon

½ tsp dried oregano

salt and freshly ground black pepper

2 medium carrots, halved and thinly sliced

¼ lb fresh stringless green beans, cut into ½ in lengths

2 small potatoes, peeled and diced

2 celery stalks, halved lengthways and thinly sliced

1 zucchini, thinly sliced into rounds

1 small eggplant, halved and thinly sliced

1 small red onion, thinly sliced

1 small cauliflower, broken into florets

½ red bell pepper, cored, seeded and cut into strips

½ green bell pepper, cored, seeded and cut into strips

¾ cup shelled fresh peas

NUTRITION FACTS	
Amount per Serving	
Calories 192	Calories from Fat 108
	% Daily Value
Total Fat 12g	18%
Saturated Fat 2g	10%
Polyunsaturated Fat 2g	0%
Monounsaturated Fat 8g	0%
Cholesterol 0mg	0%
Sodium 26mg	1%
Total Carbohydrate 15g	5%
Dietary Fiber 8g	32%
Sugars 9g	0%
Protein 6g	0%

Percent daily values are based on a 2000 calorie diet

SIDE DISHES

Mushroom, Pear, Green Bean, and Walnut Salad

Hot Beet in Yogurt and Mustard Sauce

Eggplant Dip with Sunflower Seeds

Japanese-style Vegetable Tempura

Navy Beans with Tomato Sauce and Onion

Paprika Potatoes in Spicy Sauce

Cabbage and Mint Salad

Sweet and Sour Red Cabbage

Vegetable Medley à la Greque

Glazed Carrots with Cilantro

Indian-style Vegetables

Spicy Green Beans

Pineapple and Chili Pepper Rice

Green Beans, Tomato, and Garlic

Zucchini with Walnuts

Moroccan Carrot Salad

Spicy Indian-style Potatoes

Savory Sprouts and Avocado

MUSHROOM, PEAR , GREEN BEAN, AND WALNUT SALAD

SERVES 6

This mixed fruit, vegetable, and nut salad, with its sweet-and-sour dressing, makes a substantial accompaniment to a plain dish but can also be served alone as a first course.

¼ lb green beans, trimmed and halved

2 ripe pears, peeled, cored, and sliced

2 tsp lemon juice

½ lb button mushrooms, trimmed, halved, or sliced

1 small bibb lettuce, washed, and drained and torn into small pieces

½ cup walnut halves

Dressing

1 tbsp sunflower oil

3 tbsp plain low-fat yogurt

1 tbsp clear honey

salt and freshly ground black pepper

NUTRITION FACTS

Amount per Serving
Calories 131   Calories from Fat 72

	% Daily Value
Total Fat 8g	12%
Saturated Fat 1g	5%
Polyunsaturated Fat 5g	0%
Monounsaturated Fat 1g	0%
Cholesterol 1mg	0.3%
Sodium 18mg	0.75%
Total Carbohydrate 12g	4%
Dietary Fiber 3.5g	14%
Sugars 12g	0%
Protein 3g	0%

Percent daily values are based on a 2000 calorie diet

≈ Cook the green beans in boiling water for 2 minutes, then drain them in a colander. Run cold water through them to prevent further cooking, then drain again.

≈ Sprinkle the pear slices with the lemon juice, then toss them in a bowl with the beans, mushroom, lettuce, and walnuts.

≈ Mix the dressing ingredients, pour over the salad, and toss thoroughly.

Serve.

HOT BEET IN YOGURT AND MUSTARD SAUCE

SERVES 4

A popular salad vegetable in many countries, beets have an equally attractive role to play as a hot vegetable accompaniment. This dish has middle-European origins.

1 lb small beets, trimmed and
    scrubbed

salt

⅔ cup low-fat yogurt

1 tsp cornstarch

2 tsp wholegrain mustard

1 clove garlic, crushed

1 tbsp chopped mint

freshly ground black pepper

Garnish

2 scallions, trimmed and thinly sliced

≈ Cook the beets in boiling salted water for 30 minutes, or until they are tender. Drain them and, as soon as they are cool enough to handle, scrape them. If the vegetables are very small, they are best left whole; others may be sliced or diced.

≈ Mix the yogurt with the cornstarch, and put in a pan with the mustard and garlic. Heat gently, then stir in the beets. When they have heated through, stir in the mint and season with pepper. Serve warm in a heated dish, garnished with the scallion slices.

NUTRITION FACTS	
Amount per Serving	
Calories 76	Calories from Fat 9
	% Daily Value
Total Fat 1g	1.5%
Saturated Fat 0.2g	1%
Polyunsaturated Fat 0.2g	0%
Monounsaturated Fat 0.3g	0%
Cholesterol 2mg	0.6%
Sodium 148mg	6%
Total Carbohydrate 14g	5%
Dietary Fiber 3g	12%
Sugars 11g	0%
Protein 4g	0%

Percent daily values are based on a 2000 calorie diet

EGGPLANT DIP WITH SUNFLOWER SEEDS

SERVES 4

1 tbsp sunflower seeds

1 cup grated eggplant

2–3 garlic cloves, crushed

pinch of salt

3–4 tbsp skimmed milk

1 cup low-fat plain yogurt

1 tsp artificial sweetener

¼ tsp cumin seeds, crushed

¼ tsp freshly ground black pepper

⅓ cup chopped tomato

few mint leaves or pinch of dried
    mint

pinch of chili powder

NUTRITION FACTS	
Amount per Serving	
Calories 74	Calories from Fat 27
	% Daily Value
Total Fat 3g	5%
Saturated Fat 0.5g	2.5%
Polyunsaturated Fat 1g	0%
Monounsaturated Fat 0.5g	0%
Cholesterol 3mg	1%
Sodium 63mg	3%
Total Carbohydrate 8g	3%
Dietary Fiber 2g	8%
Sugars 7g	0%
Protein 5g	0%

Percent daily values are based on a 2000 calorie diet

≈ Put the sunflower seeds into a heavy-bottomed skillet and heat them over a medium heat. Move the seeds around continuously with a wooden spoon, roasting them for 1 minute. Switch the heat off, but keep on stirring the seeds as the pan cools, then leave them to cool completely.

≈ Pour ¼ cup of water into a small saucepan, together with the eggplant, garlic, and a pinch of salt, then bring it to a boil. Cook for 2 to 3 minutes, until the eggplant is softened to a pulp, then remove the pan from the heat and leave it to one side to cool.

≈ Beat the milk and yogurt together in a bowl until smooth, then add the eggplant, sugar, cumin seeds, and pepper and blend well.

≈ Add the tomato and mint leaves or dried mint.

≈ Sprinkle the chili powder over the top and garnish with the sunflower seeds just before serving.

JAPANESE-STYLE VEGETABLE TEMPURA

SERVES 6

Maximize the color and texture of a variety of vegetables in this crisp Japanese dish. It can be served to complement baked or broiled dishes, or presented as the main dish with brown rice.

Sauce

2 in piece fresh root ginger, peeled and grated

2 tbsp soy sauce

1 tsp clear honey

⅝ cup boiling water

Vegetables

1½ cup cauliflower florets

2 large carrots, scraped and cut into julienne strips

1 large onion, sliced into rings

1 red bell pepper, cored, seeded, and sliced

¼ lb small button mushrooms, trimmed and halved

flour, for coating

sunflower oil, for deep frying

Batter

1 scant cup whole-wheat flour

2 tbsp fine cornmeal

2 tbsp arrowroot

1¼ cup water

≈ First make the sauce. Place the ginger, soy sauce, and honey in a flameproof serving bowl, pour on the boiling water, and stir well. Leave to cool.

≈ To make the batter, mix the dry ingredients in a bowl and gradually pour on the water, beating all the time.

≈ Toss all the vegetables in flour to coat them; shake off any excess. Heat the oil in a wok or deep-frying pan.

≈ Using a slotted spoon, dip the vegetables in the batter a few at a time, and allow the excess to drain back into the bowl. Fry the vegetables in several batches, reheating the oil between each one, until they are evenly golden brown.

≈ Lift out the vegetables and toss them on crumpled paper towels to drain off excess oil. Serve at once with the sauce in a separate dish.

NUTRITION FACTS	
Amount per Serving	
Calories 225	Calories from Fat 90
	% Daily Value
Total Fat 10g	15%
Saturated Fat 1g	5%
Polyunsaturated Fat 6g	0%
Monounsaturated Fat 2g	0%
Cholesterol 0mg	0%
Sodium 12mg	0.5%
Total Carbohydrate 30g	10%
Dietary Fiber 5g	20%
Sugars 6g	0%
Protein 4.5g	0%

Percent daily values are based on a 2000 calorie diet

NAVY BEANS WITH TOMATO SAUCE AND ONION

SERVES 4

This recipe is distinguished from other beans in tomato sauce recipes by the addition of a mound of finely chopped raw onion and some chopped cilantro or parsley to each portion as it is served. This really livens up the dish, but it is important to use a mild onion.

8 oz navy beans, soaked overnight and drained

3 tbsp virgin olive oil

3 garlic cloves, finely chopped

3 tbsp chopped parsley

1 tbsp chopped mixed thyme and rosemary

1 bay leaf

pinch of dried oregano

¼–½ tsp crushed red chili pepper flakes

1 cup water

2 large tomatoes, peeled, seeded, and diced

salt and freshly ground black pepper

¼ Spanish onion, very finely chopped

finely chopped cilantro or parsley, to serve

≈ Put the beans into a saucepan and just cover with water. Boil for 10 minutes and then simmer for about 50 minutes or until the beans are tender.

≈ Heat the oil, garlic, herbs, and crushed red pepper gently for 4 minutes. Add the water, bring to a boil, then cover and simmer for 5 minutes. Stir in the tomatoes, cover again and simmer for 4 minutes.

≈ Drain the beans and stir into the tomato mixture gently. Season and simmer for 4–5 minutes.

≈ Ladle the beans and sauce into four warmed soup plates and put a small mound of onion and some cilantro or parsley in the center of each.

NUTRITION FACTS

Amount per Serving

Calories 252	Calories from Fat 80
	% Daily Value
Total Fat 9g	14%
Saturated Fat 1g	5%
Polyunsaturated Fat 1g	0%
Monounsaturated Fat 6g	0%
Cholesterol 0mg	0%
Sodium 30mg	1%
Total Carbohydrate 31g	10%
Dietary Fiber 14.5g	58%
Sugars 4g	0%
Protein 13g	0%

Percent daily values are based on a 2000 calorie diet

PAPRIKA POTATOES IN SPICY SAUCE

SERVES 6

The potatoes can be pre-cooked and left in the spicy sauce, ready to be reheated while the main dish is cooking.

2¼ lb potatoes, scrubbed

salt

1 tsp sunflower oil

1 medium onion, chopped

1 clove garlic, crushed

1 tbsp paprika

1¼ cup vegetable stock

8-oz can tomatoes, chopped

½ tsp caraway seeds

1 small green bell pepper, cored, seeded, and chopped

freshly ground black pepper

3 tbsp plain low-fat yogurt

Garnish

2 tbsp chopped parsley

≈ Cook the potatoes in boiling salted water for 5 minutes, then drain them. Unless they are very small, cut the potatoes into medium-sized slices.

≈ Heat the oil in a saucepan, and fry the onion and garlic over medium heat for about 3 minutes, until the onion is soft. Stir in the paprika, and cook for 1 minute. Pour on the stock, and add the tomatoes (including juice), caraway seeds, and green bell pepper. Season with salt and pepper, add the potatoes, and stir well. Bring to a boil and simmer, uncovered, for 20 minutes, until the potatoes are tender and the sauce has thickened.

≈ Stir in the yogurt, taste the sauce, and adjust the seasoning if necessary. Serve hot, sprinkled with the parsley.

NUTRITION FACTS	
Amount per Serving	
Calories 153	Calories from Fat 9
	% Daily Value
Total Fat 1g	1.5%
Saturated Fat 0.2g	1%
Polyunsaturated Fat 0.6g	0%
Monounsaturated Fat 0.2g	0%
Cholesterol 1mg	0.3%
Sodium 40mg	2%
Total Carbohydrate 33g	11%
Dietary Fiber 4g	16%
Sugars 4.5g	0%
Protein 5g	0%

Percent daily values are based on a 2000 calorie diet

CABBAGE AND MINT SALAD

SERVES 6

Cabbage is a staple of the former Soviet Union, but in the south the spicing is notably different, and sour cream gives way to yogurt, when used. This is a cool, refreshing "coleslaw" served as a zakuska or to accompany a picnic or outdoor meal.

1½ tbsp lemon juice

2 tbsp white-wine vinegar

1½ tbsp sunflower or olive oil

½ tsp sugar

freshly ground black pepper

1 large red onion

2½ lb white cabbage

6 tbsp finely shredded fresh mint

≈ Beat together the lemon juice and vinegar in a large bowl. Whisk in the oil, sugar, and a generous dash of pepper. Halve and finely slice all but one-quarter of the red onion. Stir the onion slices into the dressing, and wrap the remaining section in aluminum foil.

· Then gently toss the shredded cabbage
· and mint leaves in the dressing.
· Combine thoroughly, and chill for at
· least 3 hours.
· ≈ Just before serving, slice the reserved
· onion and sprinkle over the salad.
·

NUTRITION FACTS	
Amount per Serving	
Calories 89	Calories from Fat 27
	% Daily Value
Total Fat 3g	5%
Saturated Fat 0.4g	2%
Polyunsaturated Fat 0.4g	0%
Monounsaturated Fat 2g	0%
Cholesterol 0mg	0%
Sodium 15mg	0.6%
Total Carbohydrate 12g	4%
Dietary Fiber 6g	24%
Sugars 12g	0%
Protein 3g	0%

Percent daily values are based on a 2000 calorie diet

SWEET AND SOUR RED CABBAGE

SERVES 6

Cabbage is an important ingredient in many kitchens, especially in Russia and Central Europe. This braised sweet-and-sour cabbage dish is also delicious served cold. If you want to make the green cabbage version, use white-wine vinegar or lemon juice and white sugar.

2 tbsp vegetable oil

1 onion, cut in half and thinly sliced

2 dessert apples, peeled, cored, and
    thinly sliced

1 red cabbage, about 1½ lb,
    quartered, cored, and shredded

¼ cup red-wine vinegar

2 to 3 tbsp light brown sugar

½ cup vegetable stock or water

salt and freshly ground black pepper

≈ In a large, heavy-bottomed, non-aluminum pan, over medium-high heat, heat oil. Add onion and cook until soft and golden, 5–7 minutes. Add sliced apples and cook until beginning to brown, 2–3 minutes.

· ≈ Add cabbage and remaining
· ingredients. Simmer, covered, stirring
· occasionally and adding water if
· necessary until cabbage is tender, 30–40
· minutes. Uncover and cook until liquid
· is absorbed. Spoon into a serving bowl.

NUTRITION FACTS	
Amount per Serving	
Calories 108	Calories from Fat 36
	% Daily Value
Total Fat 4g	6%
Saturated Fat 0.4g	2%
Polyunsaturated Fat 2.5g	0%
Monounsaturated Fat 0.5g	0%
Cholesterol 0mg	0%
Sodium 16mg	0.6%
Total Carbohydrate 17g	6%
Dietary Fiber 5g	20%
Sugars 17g	0%
Protein 2g	0%

Percent daily values are based on a 2000 calorie diet

VEGETABLE MEDLEY À LA GREQUE

SERVES 4

The joy of a dish like this one – a medley of vegetables simmered in a spicy sauce – is that you can use any seasonal produce and blend small quantities of more expensive types with plentiful, inexpensive ones.

2 small celery hearts, outer stalks removed, cut into 1-inch slices

¾ lb carrots, scraped and cut into julienne strips

½ lb snow peas, trimmed

¼ lb small onions or shallots, peeled and left whole

2 tbsp chopped cilantro, or mint

Sauce

4 tbsp tomato paste

⅝ cup dry cider

⅝ cup water

2 cloves garlic, finely chopped

1 tbsp sunflower oil

1 tsp mustard seed, lightly crushed

salt and freshly ground black pepper

1 bay leaf

≈ Put all the sauce ingredients into a pan, bring to a boil, cover and simmer for 20 minutes, until the liquid has reduced and slightly thickened.

≈ Add the celery, carrots, snow peas, and onions, bring the sauce to a boil, cover the pan, and simmer for 10 minutes or until the vegetables are tender. Remove the bay leaf and stir in half the chopped herb.

≈ Serve warm as an accompaniment to a main dish, or warm or cold as a first course. Sprinkle with the remaining herb before serving.

NUTRITION FACTS	
Amount per Serving	
Calories 114	Calories from Fat 32
	% Daily Value
Total Fat 3.5g	5%
Saturated Fat 0.5g	2.5%
Polyunsaturated Fat 2g	0%
Monounsaturated Fat 0.75g	0%
Cholesterol 0mg	0%
Sodium 107mg	4%
Total Carbohydrate 15g	5%
Dietary Fiber 7g	28%
Sugars 13g	0%
Protein 4g	0%

Percent daily values are based on a 2000 calorie diet

GLAZED CARROTS WITH CILANTRO

SERVES 4

There's a special affinity between carrots and oranges – and it's not just because of their color. This is a minus-the-fat version of glazed carrots, pepped up with ground coriander seeds.

1¼ lb carrots, scraped and cut into
   julienne strips
4 celery stalks, thinly sliced
juice and grated rind of ½ orange
⅜ cup vegetable stock
1 tsp coriander seeds, lightly crushed
salt and freshly ground black pepper

Garnish
1 tbsp chopped cilantro or mint

≈ Put the carrots, celery, orange juice and rind, stock, and coriander seeds into a pan, and season with salt and pepper. Bring to a boil and simmer uncovered over a low heat for 15 minutes or until the vegetables are tender and most of the liquid has been absorbed. Take care that the pan does not dry out. If it does, add a little more orange juice or stock.
≈ Sprinkle with the chopped herb and serve hot.

NUTRITION FACTS	
Amount per Serving	
Calories 52	Calories from Fat 5
	% Daily Value
Total Fat 0.5g	0.8%
Saturated Fat 0.1g	0.5%
Polyunsaturated Fat 0.3g	0%
Monounsaturated Fat 0g	0%
Cholesterol 0mg	0%
Sodium 53mg	2%
Total Carbohydrate 12g	4%
Dietary Fiber 5g	20%
Sugars 11g	0%
Protein 1g	0%

Percent daily values are based on a 2000 calorie diet

INDIAN-STYLE VEGETABLES

SERVES 4

¼ lb cauliflower

¼ lb green beans

¼ lb red and green bell peppers

3 tbsp oil

3–4 whole dried chili peppers,
    broken roughly

1 tsp cumin seeds

¼ tsp turmeric

½ tsp salt

¼ lb carrots

heaped ⅓ cup chopped tomatoes

2 tsp grated ginger root

3–4 plump cloves garlic, chopped or
    crushed

1 green chili pepper, chopped

2–3 tbsp chopped cilantro leaves

NUTRITION FACTS

Amount per Serving	
Calories 111	Calories from Fat 80

	% Daily Value
Total Fat 9g	14%
Saturated Fat 1g	5%
Polyunsaturated Fat 6g	0%
Monounsaturated Fat 2g	0%
Cholesterol 0mg	0%
Sodium 12mg	0.5%
Total Carbohydrate 6g	2%
Dietary Fiber 3g	12%
Sugars 5g	0%
Protein 2g	0%

Percent daily values are based on a 2000 calorie diet

≈ Cut the cauliflower into small florets.

≈ Trim the green beans and cut each one into 3–4 pieces.

≈ Cut the red and green bell peppers into small squares.

≈ Scrub and dice the carrots.

≈ Heat the oil in a medium-sized heavy-bottomed pan, then add the whole dried chili peppers, breaking them into the pan, and the cumin seeds. As they begin to sizzle, add the turmeric and salt. Stir, then add all the vegetables, including the tomato. Mix and simmer for 2 minutes.

≈ Add the ginger, garlic, and green chilies and stir to blend everything together thoroughly.

≈ Then, lower the heat, cover the pan tightly and steam cook the vegetables for 12–15 minutes.

≈ Add the cilantro leaves and serve.

SPICY GREEN BEANS

SERVES 4

Marinate these beans early in the day, and you'll have a spicy dish by dinner. These make an easy addition to a picnic or tailgate party.

≈ Cook the green beans in boiling water until just tender, 3–4 minutes. Drain and plunge into cold water, then drain well again.

≈ In a glass dish, or other non-reactive dish, whisk together all the remaining ingredients. Add the beans and stir to coat thoroughly. Refrigerate at least 3 hours. Serve cold.

1 lb fresh green beans, topped and tailed
2 tbsp vegetable oil
2 tbsp white-wine vinegar
1 tbsp fresh-squeezed lemon juice
1 tsp Creole mustard
1 garlic clove, finely chopped
1 scallion, finely chopped
1 tsp red chili pepper flakes
¼ tsp salt

NUTRITION FACTS	
Amount per Serving	
Calories 79	Calories from Fat 54

	% Daily Value
Total Fat 6g	9%
Saturated Fat 1g	15%
Polyunsaturated Fat 4g	0%
Monounsaturated Fat 1g	0%
Cholesterol 0mg	0%
Sodium 15mg	0.6%
Total Carbohydrate 4g	1%
Dietary Fiber 3.5g	14%
Sugars 3g	0%
Protein 2g	0%

Percent daily values are based on a 2000 calorie diet

PINEAPPLE AND CHILI PEPPER RICE

SERVES 4

1 large or 2 medium fresh pineapples

2 tbsp sunflower oil

1 red bell pepper, seeded, and
     chopped

8 oz zucchini, trimmed and diced

6 scallions, trimmed and sliced
     diagonally

10 oz cooked long-grain rice

6 jarred jalapeño chili peppers,
     drained and chopped

salt and freshly ground black pepper

2 tbsp pine nuts, toasted

3 tbsp freshly chopped cilantro

grated low-fat cheese, to serve

≈ Cut the pineapple in half lengthways through the plume and scoop out the flesh. Reserve the two halves. Discard the central core, dice the remaining flesh and reserve.

≈ Heat the oil in a pan and sauté the red bell pepper and zucchini for 5 minutes, or until softened. Add the scallions and sauté for a further minute. Stir the rice with the chili peppers, seasoning, and the reserved pineapple flesh.

≈ Heat gently, stirring occasionally, for 5 minutes, or until hot. Then stir in the pine nuts and cilantro. Pile into the reserved pineapple shells and serve with grated low-fat cheese.

NUTRITION FACTS	
Amount per Serving	
Calories 267	Calories from Fat 80
	% Daily Value
Total Fat 9g	14%
Saturated Fat 1g	5%
Polyunsaturated Fat 5g	0%
Monounsaturated Fat 2g	0%
Cholesterol 2mg	0.6%
Sodium 9mg	0.4%
Total Carbohydrate 42g	14%
Dietary Fiber 4.5g	18%
Sugars 19g	0%
Protein 7g	0%

Percent daily values are based on a 2000 calorie diet

GREEN BEANS, TOMATO, AND GARLIC

SERVES 4

1 tbsp vegetable oil

1 onion, finely chopped

4 cloves garlic, finely chopped

3 large green chili peppers, seeded
and sliced thinly diagonally

1 tsp ground coriander

½ tsp ground cumin

2 ripe tomatoes, blanched, skinned,
seeded, and chopped roughly

1 lb green beans, washed, trimmed,
and halved

½ tsp sugar

pinch of salt

2 tbsp fresh cilantro, chopped

NUTRITION FACTS	
Amount per Serving	
Calories 72	Calories from Fat 32
	% Daily Value
Total Fat 3.5g	5%
Saturated Fat 0.5g	2.5%
Polyunsaturated Fat 2g	0%
Monounsaturated Fat 0.5g	0%
Cholesterol 0mg	0%
Sodium 5mg	0.2%
Total Carbohydrate 7g	2%
Dietary Fiber 4.5g	18%
Sugars 6g	0%
Protein 3g	0%
Percent daily values are based on a 2000 calorie diet	

≈ Heat the oil in a wok and stir-fry the onion, garlic, and green chili peppers, stirring constantly, for 2 minutes.

≈ Add the coriander and cumin, stir vigorously and add the chopped tomatoes and beans. Stir and cover the wok for 5 minutes. Remove the cover, add the sugar and a little salt, and stir again for 1 minute. Add the cilantro, stir for 30 seconds and transfer to a warm serving dish.

ZUCCHINI WITH WALNUTS

SERVES 4

2 tbsp olive oil

1½ lb zucchini, washed, trimmed, and thinly sliced

salt and freshly ground black pepper

¾ cup walnut halves, chopped

large pinch of allspice

2 tbsp finely chopped parsley

≈ Heat the oil in a heavy skillet and sauté the zucchini, stirring it, for about 5 minutes, or until soft. Season with salt and pepper, then stir in the walnuts and allspice.

≈ Combine, take off the heat and scatter the parsley on top. Serve immediately.

NUTRITION FACTS	
Amount per Serving	
Calories 166	Calories from Fat 135
	% Daily Value
Total Fat 15g	23%
Saturated Fat 2g	10%
Polyunsaturated Fat 7g	0%
Monounsaturated Fat 6g	0%
Cholesterol 0mg	0%
Sodium 3mg	0.1%
Total Carbohydrate 3.5g	1%
Dietary Fiber 2g	8%
Sugars 3g	0%
Protein 5g	0%

Percent daily values are based on a 2000 calorie diet

MOROCCAN CARROT SALAD

SERVES 4

This is a favorite Middle Eastern salad, popular in Israel. It is sweet and spicy, as well as being colorful. Raw grated carrots can be used, but traditionally the carrots are cooked first.

1 lb carrots, peeled and cooked until just tender, cooking liquid reserved

2 tbsp vegetable oil

2 garlic cloves, peeled and finely chopped

1 tsp salt

1½ tsp cumin

½ tsp red chili pepper flakes, cayenne pepper, or red pepper sauce

1 tsp sugar

2 to 3 tbsp chopped fresh parsley

3 to 4 tbsp lemon juice

Garnish

fresh parsley sprigs

≈ In a food processor fitted with a grater blade, or with a hand-grater, grate carrots into a large bowl. Set aside.

≈ In a medium skillet, over medium-low heat, heat oil. Add chopped garlic and cook until garlic begins to soften and color, 2–3 minutes. Add salt, cumin, red chili pepper flakes, cayenne or red pepper sauce, and sugar, stirring to blend.

≈ Stir in chopped parsley and lemon juice. Slowly pour in ½–¾ cup of the carrot cooking liquid. Bring to a boil and simmer 3–5 minutes. Pour over carrots. Cool to room temperature.

≈ Cover and refrigerate 6–8 hours or overnight. Spoon into a serving bowl and garnish with parsley sprigs.

NUTRITION FACTS	
Amount per Serving	
Calories 97	Calories from Fat 54
	% Daily Value
Total Fat 6g	9%
Saturated Fat 1g	5%
Polyunsaturated Fat 4g	0%
Monounsaturated Fat 1g	0%
Cholesterol 0mg	0%
Sodium 28mg	1%
Total Carbohydrate 11g	4%
Dietary Fiber 4g	16%
Sugars 10g	0%
Protein 1g	0%

Percent daily values are based on a 2000 calorie diet

SPICY INDIAN-STYLE POTATOES

SERVES 6

This is a typical dish made by the Bene Israel Jews, who live in Bombay. The addition of green peas gives color.

3 lb waxy new or red potatoes, unpeeled and chopped

4 tbsp vegetable oil

salt

½ tsp turmeric

½ tsp ground cumin

½ tsp chili powder

½ tsp red chili pepper flakes, or ¼ tsp cayenne pepper

½ tsp curry powder or garam masala

2 tsp lemon juice

1 cup green peas (optional)

Garnish

fresh cilantro leaves (optional)

≈ Place potatoes in a large pot. Cover with cold water and, over high heat, bring to a boil. Simmer until just tender, about 20 minutes; do not overcook. Drain potatoes and rinse under cold running water to cool slightly.

≈ Peel potatoes and cut into 1-inch cubes. In a large skillet, over medium-high heat, heat 4 tablespoons oil. Add salt to taste, turmeric, cumin, chili powder, red chili pepper flakes or cayenne, and curry powder or garam masala; stir until well blended.

≈ Add potato cubes and stir to coat with spice mixture, adding a little more oil if necessary. Add lemon juice and ¼ cup water. Cook, covered, 5 minutes.

≈ Uncover and stir in the peas, if using. Cook 2–3 minutes longer until peas heat through. Serve garnished with cilantro leaves if desired.

NUTRITION FACTS	
Amount per Serving	
Calories 252	Calories from Fat 72
	% Daily Value
Total Fat 8g	12%
Saturated Fat 1g	5%
Polyunsaturated Fat 5g	0%
Monounsaturated Fat 1.5g	0%
Cholesterol 0mg	0%
Sodium 28mg	1%
Total Carbohydrate 42g	14%
Dietary Fiber 4.5g	18%
Sugars 4g	0%
Protein 5g	0%

Percent daily values are based on a 2000 calorie diet

SAVORY SPROUTS WITH AVOCADO

SERVES 4

Brussels sprouts have a very frumpy image, mainly from their association with soggy overcooked vegetables served at Christmas. Lightly boiled or steamed, so that they still have a bit of crunch, sprouts are good with traditional meals and they are also versatile ingredients for the more adventurous cook. Serve this tempting mixture as a side dish, or use it to top rice or other grains, such as couscous.

1½ lb Brussels sprouts

1 tbsp oil

1 onion, chopped

1 garlic clove, crushed (optional)

3 tbsp pine nuts or split blanched almonds

1 tsp dried oregano

3 tbsp raisins

salt and freshly ground black pepper

2 ripe avocados

juice of ½ lemon

2 tbsp chopped mint or parsley

≈ Halve the sprouts unless they are very small. Add them to a small amount of boiling water, bring back to a boil and cook for 2–3 minutes, then drain and set aside.

≈ Heat the oil. Add the onion, garlic, if used, pine nuts, oregano, and raisins with a good dash of seasoning. Cook over moderate heat, stirring often, for about 15 minutes, or until the onion is softened.

· ≈ Meanwhile, halve the avocados and
· remove their pits, then quarter the flesh
· and remove the peel. Cut into chunks
· and toss in the lemon juice.
· ≈ Add the sprouts to the onion mixture
· and cook, stirring, for about 2 minutes,
· until they are really hot. Stir in the
· avocados and parsley, or mint, then
· cook, stirring, for about 3 minutes, or
· until the avocado is hot and slightly
· creamy. Serve at once.

89

NUTRITION FACTS	
Amount per Serving	
Calories 301	Calories from Fat 216
	% Daily Value
Total Fat 24g	37%
Saturated Fat 4g	20%
Polyunsaturated Fat 8g	0%
Monounsaturated Fat 11g	0%
Cholesterol 0mg	0%
Sodium 17mg	0.7%
Total Carbohydrate 12.5g	4%
Dietary Fiber 2g	8%
Sugars 9g	0%
Protein 9g	0%

Percent daily values are based on a 2000 calorie diet

DESSERTS

Apricot Ring Mold

Blackcurrant Sorbet

Baked Rhubarb with Oat Topping

Sliced Exotic Fruits with Dates

Orange Sorbet

Apricot Praline Pavlova

Pineapple Meringue

Summer Pudding

Dairy Molds

Mixed Fruit Compote

Melon and Walnut Compote

Yogurt Delight

Pears with Cassis

Strawberry Terrine

Blackberry and Whisky Oatie

APRICOT RING MOLD

SERVES 6

With its golden color and glistening texture, this is a very appealing dessert, and one that has the hidden benefit of a high fiber content provided by the apricots.

⅓ cup light brown unrefined sugar

1 small orange

1 pt water

1 lb cooking apples, peeled, cored, and sliced

¾ lb dried apricot pieces, soaked overnight and drained

2 tbsp powdered gelatin

Decoration

herb leaves

NUTRITION FACTS

Amount per Serving	
Calories 181	Calories from Fat 5
	% Daily Value
Total Fat 0.5g	0.8%
Saturated Fat 0g	0%
Polyunsaturated Fat 0g	0%
Monounsaturated Fat 0g	0%
Cholesterol 0mg	0%
Sodium 48mg	2%
Total Carbohydrate 41g	14%
Dietary Fiber 8g	32%
Sugars 41g	0%
Protein 6g	0%

Percent daily values are based on a 2000 calorie diet

≈ Put the sugar, a strip of the orange rind, and the water in a pan and bring it slowly to a boil, stirring occasionally to dissolve the sugar. Fast-boil for 3 minutes, and then add the apple slices and poach them over low heat for about 8 minutes, or until they become translucent and are just tender. Lift out the apple slices with a slotted spoon and set them aside.

≈ Add the apricots and the juice of the orange to the syrup, bring to a boil, and simmer for 20 minutes or until the fruit is tender. Discard the orange rind, and purée the fruit thoroughly in a blender or food processor.

≈ Sprinkle the gelatin on to 3 tablespoons of hot water in a small bowl. Stand the bowl in a pan of hot water, and stir to dissolve the crystals. Stir the solution into the apricot purée and set aside to cool.

≈ Rinse a 2-pint ring mold with cold water. Arrange the apple slices in the base, and spoon on the apricot purée. Cover the mold and chill it in the refrigerator for about 2 hours, or until it has set firmly.

≈ Run a knife around the sides of the mold, and dip it quickly in and out of hot water. Place a flat serving plate over the mold, invert it quickly, and shake to release the fruit. Decorate the mold with herb leaves.

BLACKCURRANT SORBET

SERVES 4

It is reassuring to have a fruit sorbet stored in the freezer, a luxurious standby for unexpected visitors for dinner or an extra-busy occasion.

≈ Put the blackcurrants, honey, sugar, and water into a saucepan, and bring slowly to a boil, stirring occasionally. Simmer for 15 minutes, or until the fruit is soft. Allow to cool.

≈ Rub the fruit and juice through a sieve, and place it in a metal ice-cube tray or a plastic freezer box. Cover with foil or a lid, and freeze for 1–2 hours, until the mixture is mushy and starting to set on the outside.

≈ Beat the egg whites until stiff. Turn the fruit purée out into a chilled bowl and fold in the egg whites.

≈ Return the mixture to the container, cover, and freeze for another 2 hours, or until firm. Stir it once or twice.

≈ To serve, allow the sorbet to soften a little in the refrigerator for about 30 minutes. Spoon or scoop it into four individual serving glasses, and top each one with a mint sprig if you wish.

1 lb blackcurrants, fresh or frozen

4 tbsp clear honey

½ cup sugar

⅝ cup water

2 egg whites

Decoration

mint sprigs (optional)

NUTRITION FACTS	
Amount per Serving	
Calories 189	Calories from Fat 0
	% Daily Value
Total Fat 0g	0%
Saturated Fat 0g	0%
Polyunsaturated Fat 0g	0%
Monounsaturated Fat 0g	0%
Cholesterol 0mg	0%
Sodium 37mg	1.5%
Total Carbohydrate 48g	16%
Dietary Fiber 5.5g	22%
Sugars 48g	0%
Protein 2.5g	0%

Percent daily values are based on a 2000 calorie diet

BAKED RHUBARB WITH OAT TOPPING

SERVES 4

*F*amily members who like old-fashioned puddings will love this sticky-toffee fruit
layer topped with a healthful and delicious crunchy oat mixture.

1 lb rhubarb, trimmed and cut into
    1-inch lengths
grated rind and juice of 1 orange
1 tbsp water
¼ cup pitted dates, chopped
2 tbsp clear honey

Topping

1½ cups whole-wheat bread crumbs
1 cup rolled oats
¼ cup polyunsaturated margarine,
    melted
¼ cup light brown unrefined sugar

≈ Set the oven to 350°F. Place the rhubarb, orange juice and rind, water, dates, and honey in a 2½ pint ovenproof dish.

≈ For the topping, mix together the bread crumbs, oats, margarine, and sugar, and spread the topping over the fruit. Bake in the oven for about 35 minutes, until the topping is golden.

Serve piping hot.

NUTRITION FACTS	
Amount per Serving	
Calories 344	Calories from Fat 126
	% Daily Value
Total Fat 14g	21%
Saturated Fat 3g	15%
Polyunsaturated Fat 6g	0%
Monounsaturated Fat 4.5g	0%
Cholesterol 0mg	0%
Sodium 230mg	9.5%
Total Carbohydrate 51g	17%
Dietary Fiber 7g	28%
Sugars 28g	0%
Protein 6g	0%

Percent daily values are based on a 2000 calorie diet

SLICED EXOTIC FRUITS WITH DATES

SERVES 6

Fruit salad has always been a popular dessert and almost any seasonal fruits are delicious sliced or cut up together in their natural juices or with a fruit purée. This is not a traditional fruit salad, but a selection of exotic fruits, sliced and served together. Ogen melons from Israel are as sweet as sugar, as are the Israeli oranges. California produces a wonderful variety of date, the Medjool date, which is recommended for this dish.

1 ogen or canteloupe melon, seeded and sliced in thin wedges and peeled

3 sweet seedless oranges, peeled and segmented, juice reserved

1 mango, peeled and thinly sliced

24 fresh lychees, peeled, or 1 16-oz can lychees in their own juice

12 Medjool dates, cut in half lengthwise and pitted

1 pomegranate, cut in half, seeds reserved (optional)

Garnish
fresh mint leaves

≈ Arrange slices of melon on each of six individual plates in a fan shape. Arrange peeled orange segments and mango slices in an attractive pattern over the melon slices.

≈ Evenly distribute fresh or canned lychees over fruit and sprinkle on some reserved juices from all fruits.

≈ Arrange four date halves on each plate and sprinkle with the pomegranate seeds, if using. Garnish with fresh mint leaves and serve.

95

ORANGE SORBET

SERVES 6

1 cup sugar

grated zest and juice of 1 lemon

grated zest of 3 oranges

2 cups fresh-squeezed orange juice, strained

2 egg whites, beaten to soft peaks

fresh mint leaves for garnish

Cointreau for serving

Citrus fruit sorbets and ices make an ideal dessert choice after any meal. Adding beaten egg whites gives sorbet a very smooth, creamy texture. If you prefer a rougher, "icier" texture, omit the whites. Processing the mixture breaks up the ice crystals and contributes to a smooth texture.

≈ In a small heavy saucepan, combine sugar, lemon and orange zests and 1 cup water. Slowly bring to a boil, stirring until sugar dissolves. Cook 5 minutes; remove from heat and cool and refrigerate 3–4 hours or overnight.

≈ Combine lemon and orange juices with the chilled syrup and, if you like, strain for a very smooth sorbet.

≈ If using an ice-cream machine, freeze according to manufacturer's directions.

≈ Alternatively, put into a metal bowl and freeze 3–4 hours until semifrozen. Into a food processor fitted with metal blade. Scrape the semifrozen mixture; process until light and creamy, 30–45 seconds. Return to the metal bowl and freeze another 1½ hours. Scrape into food processor again and process with beaten egg whites until well mixed and light and creamy, 30 seconds. Freeze 3–4 hours until completely firm.

≈ Soften 5 minutes at room temperature before scooping into individual serving glasses. Garnish with a few mint leaves and pass the liqueur, allowing each guest to pour a little over sorbet.

NUTRITION FACTS	
Amount per Serving	
Calories 178	Calories from Fat 0
	% Daily Value
Total Fat 0g	0%
Saturated Fat 0g	0%
Polyunsaturated Fat 0g	0%
Monounsaturated Fat 0g	0%
Cholesterol 0mg	0%
Sodium 24mg	1%
Total Carbohydrate 46g	15%
Dietary Fiber 1g	4%
Sugars 46g	0%
Protein 1g	0%

Percent daily values are based on a 2000 calorie diet

APRICOT PRALINE PAVLOVA

SERVES 6

A spectacular dessert to draw delighted comments at the end of a special meal, and proof that pavlova, a filled meringue basket, does not have to be filled with whipped cream.

½ lb dried apricot pieces

1¼ cup orange juice

⅝ cup plain low-fat yogurt

Praline

6 tbsp set honey

1 oz superfine sugar

4 oz chopped blanched almonds

oil, for brushing

Meringue

3 egg whites

¾ cup fine granulated sugar

≈ Soak the apricots in the orange juice for at least 2 hours, or overnight; place in a pan, bring to a boil, and simmer for 20 minutes until the fruit is tender. Allow to cool, then purée the apricots and any remaining juice in a blender or food processor and beat in the yogurt.

≈ To make the praline, put the honey and ⅛ cup sugar into a small pan and bring to a boil. Boil for 5 minutes, until very thick. Remove from the heat, and stir in the almonds. Pour into an oiled tin, and leave to cool.

≈ Set the oven to 275°F. To make the meringue, whisk the egg whites until they are very stiff. Fold in half the sugar, and whisk again until the mixture is stiff and glossy. Fold in the remaining sugar.

≈ Line a cookie sheet with waxed paper, and spoon the meringue to make a nest. Bake in the oven for 1 hour, or until the meringue is firm. Leave it to cool, then peel off the paper, and place it on a serving dish.

≈ Coarsely crush the praline with a rolling pin or in the blender. Just before serving, spoon the apricot mixture into the center of the meringue, and sprinkle on the praline.

NUTRITION FACTS

Amount per Serving

Calories 366	Calories from Fat 90
	% Daily Value
Total Fat 10g	15%
Saturated Fat 1g	5%
Polyunsaturated Fat 3g	0%
Monounsaturated Fat 6g	0%
Cholesterol 1mg	0.3%
Sodium 79mg	3%
Total Carbohydrate 64g	21%
Dietary Fiber 6g	24%
Sugars 64g	0%
Protein 8g	0%

Percent daily values are based on a 2000 calorie diet

PINEAPPLE MERINGUE

SERVES 6

Pineapple rings, broiled until they are toasty-brown and then topped with fluffy meringue, make an impressive dessert for a dinner party.

≈ Line the broiling pan with foil. In a small bowl mix together the raisins, orange juice, and orange rind, and set aside for a few minutes.

≈ Brush the pineapple rings with half the margarine, and broil them for 4–5 minutes (at medium heat), until they are brown. Turn the rings, brush the other side with the remaining margarine, and broil for another 4–5 minutes.

≈ Whisk the egg whites until they are stiff. Whisk in half the sugar, and continue beating until the mixture is stiff and glossy. Fold in the remaining sugar and the nuts.

≈ Spoon the raisin mixture into the center of the pineapple rings, and cover them with the meringue. Broil for 2–3 minutes, until the topping is streaked with brown. Serve hot.

¼ cup white seedless raisins

2 tbsp orange juice

1 tsp grated orange rind

1 pineapple, peeled, cored, and sliced into 6 rings

⅛ cup polyunsaturated margarine, melted

Meringue

2 egg whites

⅔ cup light brown sugar

2 tbsp chopped almonds, toasted

NUTRITION FACTS	
Amount per Serving	
Calories 162	Calories from Fat 54
	% Daily Value
Total Fat 6g	9%
Saturated Fat 1g	5%
Polyunsaturated Fat 2g	0%
Monounsaturated Fat 3g	0%
Cholesterol 0mg	0%
Sodium 62mg	2.5%
Total Carbohydrate 26g	9%
Dietary Fiber 1.5g	6%
Sugars 26g	0%
Protein 2g	0%

Percent daily values are based on a 2000 calorie diet

SUMMER PUDDING

SERVES 6

This traditional English pudding is a delightful way to celebrate the berry harvest or to use a store of frozen berries.

2¼ lb mixed berries such as raspberries, gooseberries and blackcurrants

¼ cup light or brown unrefined sugar, or to taste

3–4 tbsp water

about 8 slices whole-wheat bread cut from a large loaf, crusts removed

Garnish

scented herb leaves (optional)

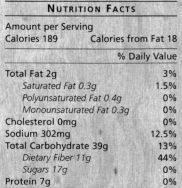

NUTRITION FACTS

Amount per Serving	
Calories 189	Calories from Fat 18
	% Daily Value
Total Fat 2g	3%
Saturated Fat 0.3g	1.5%
Polyunsaturated Fat 0.4g	0%
Monounsaturated Fat 0.3g	0%
Cholesterol 0mg	0%
Sodium 302mg	12.5%
Total Carbohydrate 39g	13%
Dietary Fiber 11g	44%
Sugars 17g	0%
Protein 7g	0%

Percent daily values are based on a 2000 calorie diet

≈ Prepare the fruit as required: hull raspberries, top and tail gooseberries, and strip blackcurrants from the stalks. Put the fruit into a large pan with the sugar and water, and cook over a low heat until the sugar dissolves and the juices start to run. Cook gently until all the fruit is just tender – about 15 minutes.

≈ Cut the bread slices to line a 2-pint bowl. Fit the bread around the container so that there are no gaps.

≈ Tip the fruit into the bowl and cover the top with more bread slices so that the fruit is completely enclosed. Place a saucer or small plate over the container and press it down with a heavy weight.

≈ Leave the pudding in the refrigerator for several hours or overnight. To unmold the pudding, run a knife blade between the bowl and the bread lining, place a serving plate over the top, invert both pudding and plate, and shake sharply to release the pudding. Decorate with the herb leaves.

DAIRY MOLDS

SERVES 6

A delicious low-fat version of the French coeur à la crème, *this dairy blend makes a light and delightful accompaniment to berries of all kinds.*

2 cups low-fat cottage cheese

⅝ cups plain low-fat yogurt

3 tbsp warm water

1 tbsp powdered gelatin

≈ Strain the cottage cheese into a bowl. Beat in the yogurt.

≈ Pour the water into a small bowl, sprinkle on the gelatin, stir well, and stand the bowl in a pan of warm water. Leave for about 5 minutes for the gelatine to dissolve. Pour the gelatin mixture into the cheese and beat well.

≈ Spoon the cheese into 6 individual molds. Heart-shaped ones are traditional, or you can improvise by using ramekin dishes or yogurt tubs covered with cheesecloth and inverted. Stand the molds on a wire rack over a plate and leave them to drain in the refrigerator overnight.

≈ Turn out the molds, and serve well chilled.

NUTRITION FACTS	
Amount per Serving	
Calories 88	Calories from Fat 9
	% Daily Value
Total Fat 1g	1.5%
Saturated Fat 1g	5%
Polyunsaturated Fat 0g	0%
Monounsaturated Fat 0g	0%
Cholesterol 5mg	1.6%
Sodium 324mg	13.5%
Total Carbohydrate 5g	1.6%
Dietary Fiber 0g	0%
Sugars 5g	0%
Protein 14.5g	0%

Percent daily values are based on a 2000 calorie diet

MIXED FRUIT COMPOTE

SERVES 10

The perfect accompaniment to this delicious dessert is low-fat yogurt.

12 oz pears

12 oz apples

12 oz peaches

12 oz apricots

2 tbsp freshly squeezed lemon juice

3½ cups superfine sugar

2 cinnamon sticks

3¾ cups water

3–4 whole cloves

strip of lemon peel

NUTRITION FACTS	
Amount per Serving	
Calories 268	Calories from Fat 1
	% Daily Value
Total Fat 0.1g	0.2%
Saturated Fat 0g	0%
Polyunsaturated Fat 0g	0%
Monounsaturated Fat 0g	0%
Cholesterol 0mg	0%
Sodium 6mg	0.25%
Total Carbohydrate 70g	2.3%
Dietary Fiber 2g	8%
Sugars 70g	0%
Protein 1g	0%

Percent daily values are based on a 2000 calorie diet

≈ To prepare the fruit for the compote, peel, core, and quarter the pears and apples. Wash the peaches and apricots, and remove the pits. Cut the peaches into quarters and the apricots in half.
≈ Place the pear and apple quarters in a large, heavy-based saucepan with the lemon juice, sugar, cinnamon sticks, water, cloves, and lemon peel. Gently bring to a boil and simmer for 5 minutes.

≈ Add the peaches and cook for a further 5 minutes, then add the apricot halves and continue to cook for 3–5 minutes or until softened. Using a slotted spoon, transfer the fruit to a serving bowl, cover, and set aside.
≈ Return the syrup to a boil and continue to boil rapidly for about 10 minutes, or until reduced slightly and thickened. Remove the cinnamon sticks, cloves, and lemon peel. Allow the syrup to cool, then pour over the fruit. Serve at room temperature or chilled.

MELON AND WALNUT COMPOTE

SERVES 6

Versions of this simple dessert are eaten from Greece through Georgia and Armenia to Uzbekistan.

2 small cantaloupe or honeydew melons, halved, seeded, and cubed

1½ cups honey

3 cups walnuts, chopped

NUTRITION FACTS	
Amount per Serving	
Calories 267	Calories from Fat 95
	% Daily Value
Total Fat 10.5g	16%
Saturated Fat 1g	5%
Polyunsaturated Fat 7g	0%
Monounsaturated Fat 2g	0%
Cholesterol 0mg	0%
Sodium 69mg	3%
Total Carbohydrate 42g	14%
Dietary Fiber 2.5g	10%
Sugars 42g	0%
Protein 3.5g	0%

Percent daily values are based on a 2000 calorie diet

≈ Place the melon cubes, with any juice, in a bowl. Add the honey and toss to coat lightly. Stir in the walnuts. Divide the mixture among individual bowls.

YOGURT DELIGHT

SERVES 4

3 cups low-fat yogurt

grated zest and juice of 1 orange

¼–⅓ cup clear honey

knob of unsalted butter

⅓ cup shelled pistachio nuts

½ cup Brazil nuts, roughly chopped

⅓ cup raisins

2 firm pears, peeled, cored and diced

¾ cup ready-to-eat dried apricots, sliced

½ cup seedless grapes, halved

NUTRITION FACTS

Amount per Serving

Calories 666	Calories from Fat 130
	% Daily Value
Total Fat 14.5g	22%
Saturated Fat 4g	20%
Polyunsaturated Fat 4g	0%
Monounsaturated Fat 5g	0%
Cholesterol 10mg	3%
Sodium 235mg	10%
Total Carbohydrate 125g	42%
Dietary Fiber 29g	116%
Sugars 125g	0%
Protein 16g	0%

Percent daily values are based on a 2000 calorie diet

≈ Mix the yogurt, orange zest, and 2–3 tbsp of the honey, then divide it between four dishes and chill well.

≈ Melt the butter, then stir fry the pistachios and Brazils with the raisins for 3 minutes. Add the pears and continue to stir fry for about 3 minutes, or until the pears are lightly cooked. Stir in the apricots and orange juice and bring to a boil. Boil, stirring, for 2 minutes to reduce the orange juice.

≈ Stir in the grapes and remaining honey (or to taste) and heat through briefly. Spoon the fruit and nut mixture on top of the chilled yogurt and serve at once.

PEARS WITH CASSIS

SERVES 4

≈ Toss the pears in the orange juice. Melt the butter, then add the pears, reserving the juice, and stir fry until they are softened but still retaining their shape.

≈ Pour the orange juice and cassis over the pears and mix well to coat all the

- pieces of fruit in sauce. Transfer to four
- dishes and sprinkle each portion with
- flaked almonds. Decorate with
- blackcurrant sprigs or halved orange
- slices when blackcurrants are not
- available. Serve at once, with low-fat
- yogurt.

8 small, firm pears, peeled, cored
   and quartered
juice of 1 large orange
1 tsp of unsalted butter
½ cup cassis (blackcurrant liqueur)
⅓ cup flaked almonds, toasted
sprigs of blackcurrants or halved
   orange slices to decorate
low-fat yogurt to serve

NUTRITION FACTS		
Amount per Serving		
Calories 238	Calories from Fat 63	
		% Daily Value
Total Fat 7g		11%
Saturated Fat 1g		5%
Polyunsaturated Fat 1.5g		0%
Monounsaturated Fat 4g		0%
Cholesterol 3mg		1%
Sodium 23mg		1%
Total Carbohydrate 43.5g		14.5%
Dietary Fiber 8g		32%
Sugars 43g		0%
Protein 3g		0%

Percent daily values are based on a 2000 calorie diet

STRAWBERRY TERRINE

SERVES 8

Ripe strawberries in a liqueur-flavored jello make a spectacular centerpiece for a dinner party or buffet table. You can substitute other berries, or carry the idea into another season and use orange sections instead.

2⅓ cups superfine sugar

thinly-grated zest of 1 orange

1¼ pt water

4 tbsp (4 envelopes) powdered gelatine

2 tbsp kirsch or brandy

2¼ lb fresh strawberries, hulled and quartered

Decoration

½ lb fresh strawberries, halved

≈ Put the sugar, orange zest, and water into a pan, and bring slowly to a boil, stirring occasionally. Boil for 5 minutes, then remove from the heat and allow to cool a little. Sprinkle on the gelatin crystals and stir well. Set aside to cool, but do not allow to set. Strain the syrup into a pitcher through a fine mesh strainer lined with paper towel, and stir in the liqueur or brandy.

≈ Rinse a 2-pint mold with cold water, and arrange the quartered strawberries to make a pattern. Slowly pour the syrup over the fruit, taking care not to displace the fruit. Cover the mold with foil and place it in the refrigerator for several hours or overnight.

≈ To unmold the terrine, run a hot knife between the gelatin and the mold and place a cloth rinsed in hot water over the base for no more than a few seconds. Place a serving plate over the mold, quickly invert the plate and the mold together, and shake sharply to release the dessert.

≈ Decorate the dessert with fresh strawberries. You can hull the fruit if you wish, but it looks more decorative and provides a natural element of contrast if you do not.

NUTRITION FACTS

Amount per Serving

Calories 292	Calories from Fat 1
	% Daily Value
Total Fat 0.15g	0.2%
Saturated Fat 0g	5%
Polyunsaturated Fat 0g	0%
Monounsaturated Fat 0g	0%
Cholesterol 0mg	0%
Sodium 29mg	1%
Total Carbohydrate 69g	23%
Dietary Fiber 2g	8%
Sugars 69g	0%
Protein 5.5g	0%

Percent daily values are based on a 2000 calorie diet

BLACKBERRY AND WHISKY OATIE

SERVES 4

This dessert has its origins in Scotland, where the combination of oats and whisky strikes a chord of national pride.

≈ Put the oats and whisky into a bowl, cover, and set aside for at least 2 hours, or overnight if it is more convenient.

≈ Beat together the honey, cheese, and yogurt and stir in the orange rind. Stir in most of the blackberries.

≈ In four tall glass dessert dishes, make layers of the fruit mixture and oats, beginning and ending with the fruit.

Decorate each glass with a few reserved berries and a sprig of fresh mint. Serve chilled.

⅔ cups rolled oat

5 tbsp Scotch whisky

3 tbsp clear honey

½ cup low-fat cottage cheese, sieved

⅝ cup plain low-fat yogurt

1 tsp grated orange rind

½ lb blackberries, hulled

Decoration

fresh mint

NUTRITION FACTS

Amount per Serving

Calories 217	Calories from Fat 23

	% Daily Value
Total Fat 2.5g	4%
Saturated Fat 0.7g	3.5%
Polyunsaturated Fat 0.7g	0%
Monounsaturated Fat 0.85g	0%
Cholesterol 3mg	1%
Sodium 131mg	5.5%
Total Carbohydrate 32g	11%
Dietary Fiber 4g	16%
Sugars 20g	0%
Protein 8g	0%

Percent daily values are based on a 2000 calorie diet

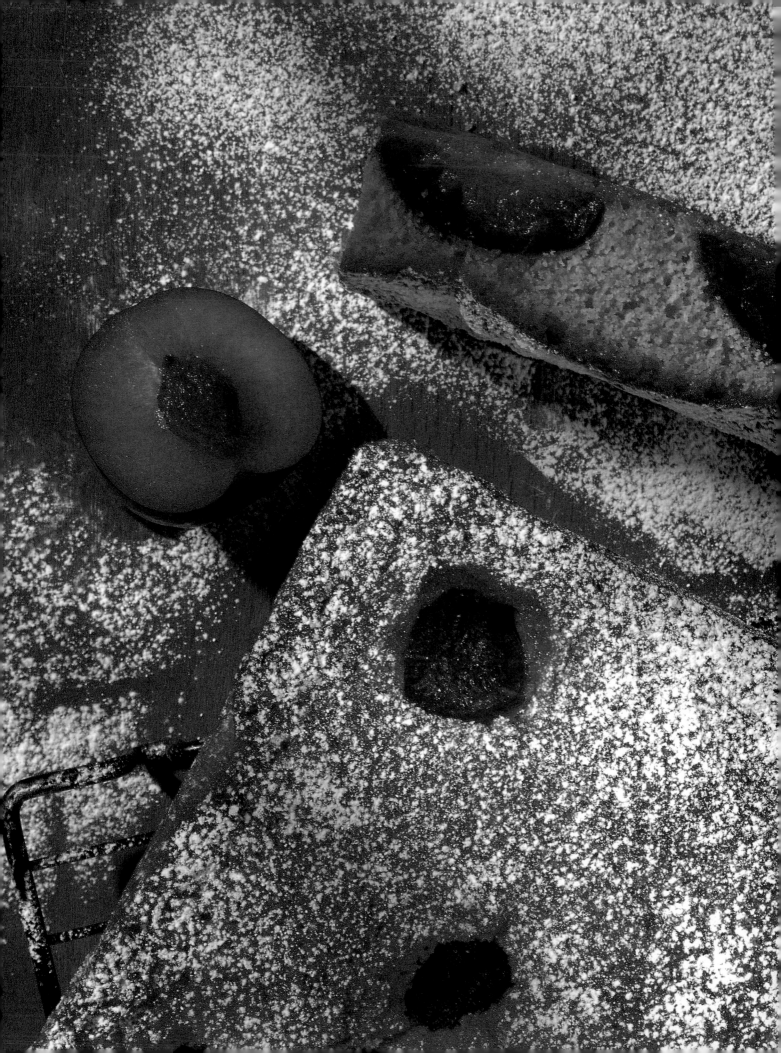

BAKED GOODS

Singing Hinny

Almond Rice Cookies

Sweet Spiced Fig Bread

Date and Orange Bars

Low-fat Spongecake

Cheese Bread

Cornbread

Herbed Biscuits

Coconut Macaroons

Easy Cinnamon Balls

Muesli Cookies

Apple Cake

Bran Fruit Loaf

Pumpkin, Sunflower Seed, and Raisin Cake

Banana, Nectarine, and Almond Loaf

Carrot and Orange Cake

SINGING HINNY

MAKES 12 SLICES

The name of this fruit scone, or shortcake, from the north of England, is said to come from the sound it makes sizzling on the griddle.

2¼ cups whole-wheat cake flour,
plus extra for dusting

1 tsp salt

⅛ cup polyunsaturated margarine

¾ cup 100% bran cereal

⅔ cup (generous) ground rice

⅓ cup (generous) unrefined brown
sugar

⅓ cup currants

⅝ cup low-fat milk

⅝ cup plain low-fat yogurt

oil, for brushing

≈ Mix the flour and salt in a bowl, and cream in the margarine until the mixture resembles fine bread crumbs. Stir in the bran cereal, rice, sugar, and currants, and mix thoroughly.

≈ Make a well in the center of the dry ingredients, and gradually mix in the milk and yogurt. Then turn out the dough onto a lightly-floured board, and knead it gently to remove any cracks.

≈ Divide the dough into two equal pieces, and roll them out to make 9-inch circles. Prick each one all over with a fork and mark into six wedges.

≈ Lightly brush a skillet or griddle with oil, and preheat it over medium heat. Cook the scone for 3–4 minutes on each side. Serve them warm, with honey or jam.

110

ALMOND RICE COOKIES

MAKES ABOUT 12 COOKIES

Using only the white of the egg and no butter or oil, these cookies fit well into a low-fat regime.

⅔ cup ground rice

2 tbsp ground almonds

¼ cup sugar

1 egg white, lightly beaten

2 tbsp clear honey

2–3 drops almond extract

12 split blanched almonds

≈ Preheat the oven to 325°F. Mix together the rice, ground almonds, and sugar. Thoroughly beat in the egg white, honey, and almond extract.

≈ Line a cookie sheet with waxed paper. Place teaspoons of the mixture well apart on the paper, and press a split almond on top of each.

≈ Bake in the oven for 15–20 minutes, until the cookies are light golden brown. Leave them to cool slightly on the cookie sheet, then lift them off the waxed paper. When cool, store in an airtight tin.

NUTRITION FACTS	
Amount per Serving (per cookie)	
Calories 73	Calories from Fat 23
	% Daily Value
Total Fat 2.5g	4%
Saturated Fat 0.2g	1%
Polyunsaturated Fat 0.6g	0%
Monounsaturated Fat 1.5g	0%
Cholesterol 0mg	0%
Sodium 6mg	0.25%
Total Carbohydrate 11g	4%
Dietary Fiber 1g	4%
Sugars 6g	0%
Protein 1.5g	0%

Percent daily values are based on a 2000 calorie diet

SWEET SPICED FIG BREAD

MAKES ONE 1 LB LOAF

Not so much a bread as a spiced tea bread which is especially good with cottage cheese and orange segments.

1 cup (scant) whole-wheat flour

2 tsp baking powder

1 tsp ground cinnamon

large pinch grated nutmeg

1⅓ cup rolled oats

½ cup (scant) light Muscovado or
  brown sugar

3 tbsp clear honey

1¼ cup skimmed milk

⅔ cup dried figs, chopped

NUTRITION FACTS	
Amount per Serving (per 1lb loaf)	
Calories 1510	Calories from Fat 135
	% Daily Value
Total Fat 15g	20%
Saturated Fat 2.5g	12.5%
Polyunsaturated Fat 5g	0%
Monounsaturated Fat 4g	0%
Cholesterol 6mg	2%
Sodium 273mg	10%
Total Carbohydrate 330g	1%
Dietary Fiber 33.5g	132%
Sugars 196g	0%
Protein 39g	0%
Percent daily values are based on a 2000 calorie diet	

≈ Preheat the oven to 350°F. Sift the flour, baking powder, and spices into a bowl, and tip in any bran (husk) remaining in the sifter. Stir in the oats, sugar, and honey, then gradually pour on the milk, beating constantly. Stir in the chopped figs.

≈ Line a 1-lb loaf tin with waxed paper, spoon in the mixture, and level the top. Bake in the oven for 50 minutes or until a skewer inserted into the loaf comes out clean.

≈ Leave the loaf to cool slightly in the pan, then turn it out onto a cake rack. When completely cool it can be wrapped in foil and stored in an airtight container.

DATE AND ORANGE BARS

MAKES 10 BARS

The zing of oranges and the sweetness of the dates make an irresistible combination.

1 cup pitted dates, chopped

grated rind of 2 oranges

1 orange, peeled, sectioned, and chopped

¼ cup polyunsaturated margarine

1⅓ cup rolled oats

⅝ cup whole-wheat flour

3 tbsp clear honey

¼ cup pecan nuts, chopped

1 tbsp sesame seeds

oil, for brushing

≈ Preheat the oven to 375°F. Mix together the dates, orange rind, and chopped orange, and set aside.

≈ Melt the margarine in a small pan and stir in the oats, flour, honey, nuts, and seeds. Lightly oil a 7-inch square cake pan.

≈ Press half the oat mixture into the pan to cover the base. Level the surface and cover it with the date mixture. Spread the remaining oat mixture on top, and press it down evenly.

≈ Bake in the oven for 25–30 minutes, until the top is golden brown. Cool slightly, then cut into ten bars. To do this, cut the cake in half, and then cut each half into five bars.

NUTRITION FACTS	
Amount per Serving (per bar)	
Calories 196	Calories from Fat 80

	% Daily Value
Total Fat 9g	0.1%
Saturated Fat 1.5g	7.5%
Polyunsaturated Fat 3.5g	0%
Monounsaturated Fat 3g	0%
Cholesterol 0mg	0%
Sodium 43mg	2%
Total Carbohydrate 28g	9%
Dietary Fiber 3g	12%
Sugars 17g	0%
Protein 3g	0%

Percent daily values are based on a 2000 calorie diet

SPONGECAKE

MAKES 6 SLICES

For this classic sponge cake no butter, margarine or oil is used in the mixture. It must be noted, however, that the use of three egg yolks contributes a significant cholesterol content. An electric beater is a great advantage.

oil, for brushing

3 large eggs

⅓ cup superfine sugar

few drops vanilla extract

⅝ cup all-purpose flour, plus extra for dusting

Filling

⅔ cup strawberry preserve

⅝ cup low-fat yogurt

Topping

3 tbsp confectioners' sugar

≈ Preheat the oven to 350°F. First prepare the pans. Lightly brush the bases of two 7-inch diameter cake pans with oil. Line the base of each pan with a circle of waxed paper, and brush that with oil. Dust the base and sides of each pan with flour. Shake off excess flour.

≈ Pour boiling water into a saucepan to a depth of 2 inches, and fit a large flameproof bowl over it. Put the pan on low heat to keep the water simmering.

≈ Put the eggs, sugar, and vanilla extract into the bowl and whisk until the mixture is very thick, and warm. A hand-held electric beater will take about 10 minutes.

≈ Remove the bowl from the heat and beat until the beaters leave a trail in the mixture and it has cooled.

≈ Gradually sift the flour, a little at a time, into the egg mixture, folding it in with a metal spoon. Divide the mixture between the two pans, and level the tops.

≈ Bake in the oven for 20–25 minutes, until the cakes have shrunk away from the sides of the pans.

≈ Leave the cakes in the pans for about 5 minutes, then turn them out onto cake racks. Peel off the paper and leave them to cool. When the cakes are cool, sandwich them together with the jam and yogurt.

JELLY ROLL

≈ You can use this mixture to make a jelly roll. Brush the pan with oil, line it with waxed paper, and brush that with oil.

≈ When the cake is cooled, turn it out onto a sheet of waxed paper sprinkled with fine granulated sugar. Place another sheet of paper on top and roll up the cake with the paper inside.

≈ Unroll the cake when it is cool, remove the paper, and spread the cake with preserve or jelly. Roll it up again and sprinkle with confectioners' sugar.

NUTRITION FACTS	
Amount per Serving (per slice)	
Calories 237	Calories from Fat 36
	% Daily Value
Total Fat 4g	6%
Saturated Fat 1g	5%
Polyunsaturated Fat 1g	0%
Monounsaturated Fat 2g	0%
Cholesterol 120mg	40%
Sodium 73mg	3%
Total Carbohydrate 47g	16%
Dietary Fiber 0.5g	2%
Sugars 39g	0%
Protein 6g	0%

Percent daily values are based on a 2000 calorie diet

CHEESE BREAD

MAKES ABOUT TWO 1-LB LOAVES (APPROX. 20 SLICES)

You can serve this lightly spiced cheese bread as a snack with a mixed green salad, celery, or a selection of raw vegetables.

≈ Mix together the flour, salt, and crushed cereal in a bowl. Rub in the margarine until the mixture resembles fine bread crumbs. Stir in the cheese, yeast, mace, and cumin seeds, and gradually pour in the water, mixing it all the time. Use just enough to give a firm and not sticky dough.

≈ Turn the dough out onto a lightly floured board, and knead it lightly to remove any cracks. Place the dough in a bowl, cover it with plastic wrap, and set it aside in a warm place to rise – 45 minutes. Knead for 1 minute.

≈ Set the oven to 450°F. Lightly brush two 1-lb loaf tins with oil. Divide the dough into two equal pieces, and press each one into a loaf tin, working it well into the corners.

≈ Bake the loaves in the oven for 5 minutes, then reduce the heat to 400°F. Continue cooking for another 30–35 minutes, until the loaves sound hollow when tapped on the bottom.

≈ Leave the loaves to cool slightly in the tins, then turn them out onto a cake rack to cool.

4⅓ cups whole-wheat flour, plus extra for dusting

2 tsp salt

1⅛ cups bran cereal, crushed

1 tbsp polyunsaturated margarine

¾ cup low-fat hard cheese, grated

4¼ tsp instant dried yeast

½ tsp dried mace

2 tsp cumin seeds

about 1 pt tepid water

oil, for brushing

NUTRITION FACTS	
Amount per Serving (per slice)	
Calories 90	Calories from Fat 18
	% Daily Value
Total Fat 2g	3%
Saturated Fat 0.6g	3%
Polyunsaturated Fat 0.6g	0%
Monounsaturated Fat 0.6g	0%
Cholesterol 2mg	0.7%
Sodium 55mg	2%
Total Carbohydrate 15g	5%
Dietary Fiber 3.5g	14%
Sugars 1.0g	0%
Protein 4g	0%

Percent daily values are based on a 2000 calorie diet

CORNBREAD

MAKES 6 SLICES

Served warm with low-fat cottage cheese and honey, this cornbread makes a good breakfast or teatime treat.

⅓ cup cornmeal

⅝ cup self-raising whole-wheat flour

½ tsp baking powder

1 tbsp polyunsaturated margarine, melted

1 small egg, lightly beaten

½ cup low-fat milk

1 tbsp clear honey

Topping

2 tbsp rolled oats

≈ Preheat the oven to 400°F. Sift the cornmeal, flour, and baking powder into a bowl, and tip in any bran (husk) remaining in the sifter. Make a well in the center of the dry ingredients.

≈ Mix together the margarine, egg, milk, and honey. Gradually incorporate the dry ingredients, beating well.

≈ Place a non-stick 8-inch flan ring on a non-stick cookie sheet (or lightly brush a non-coated one with oil). Press the mixture into the ring, mark it into six wedges and sprinkle the oats on top.

≈ Bake in the oven for 20 minutes, until well risen and springy to the touch. Cool slightly, then turn the bread out onto a cake rack. Serve warm.

NUTRITION FACTS	
Amount per Serving	
Calories 141	Calories from Fat 45
	% Daily Value
Total Fat 5g	8%
Saturated Fat 1g	5%
Polyunsaturated Fat 2g	0%
Monounsaturated Fat 2g	0%
Cholesterol 40mg	13%
Sodium 50mg	2%
Total Carbohydrate 20g	7%
Dietary Fiber 2g	8%
Sugars 3.5g	0%
Protein 5g	0%

Percent daily values are based on a 2000 calorie diet

HERBED BISCUITS

MAKES ABOUT 10 BISCUITS

These savory biscuits, eaten warm, make a good snack to enjoy with low-fat cheese or grapes and celery. They also make a good accompaniment to a bowl of steaming hot soup.

1½ cups whole-wheat flour, plus extra for dusting

½ tsp salt

½ tsp baking soda

¼ cup (scant) polyunsaturated margarine

1 tsp mixed dry herbs

1 tsp paprika

⅝ cup plain low-fat yogurt or buttermilk

milk, to glaze

≈ Preheat the oven to 400°F. Sift the flour, salt, and soda into a bowl. Rub in the margarine until the mixture resembles fine bread crumbs. Stir in the herbs and paprika, and make a well in the center of the dry ingredients. Mix in the yogurt or buttermilk to make a firm dough.

≈ Turn out the dough on to a lightly-floured board, and knead it lightly to remove any cracks. Roll it out to a thickness of about ¾ inch, then, using a fluted cutter, cut it into 2 inch circles. Re-roll the trimmings and cut into more circles. Brush the tops with milk to glaze.

≈ Place the biscuits on a non-stick cookie sheet, and bake in the oven for 20 minutes, until they are well risen and golden brown. Transfer the biscuits to a cake rack to cool slightly. Serve warm.

NUTRITION FACTS	
Amount per Serving (per biscuit)	
Calories 104	Calories from Fat 45
	% Daily Value
Total Fat 5g	8%
Saturated Fat 1g	5%
Polyunsaturated Fat 2g	0%
Monounsaturated Fat 1.5g	0%
Cholesterol 1mg	0.3%
Sodium 51mg	2%
Total Carbohydrate 12g	4%
Dietary Fiber 2g	8%
Sugars 1.5g	0%
Protein 3g	0%

Percent daily values are based on a 2000 calorie diet

COCONUT MACAROONS

MAKES ABOUT 30

Macaroons taste delicious and are a good way to use extra egg whites.

4 egg whites

¼ tsp cream of tartar

1 cup sugar

1 tsp lemon juice or distilled white
   vinegar

1 tsp vanilla extract

2½ cups moist, unsweetened
   shredded coconut

≈ In a large bowl, with electric mixer at medium speed, beat whites until frothy. Add cream of tartar and beat on high speed until firm peaks form. Gradually sprinkle in sugar, 2 tablespoons at a time, beating well after each addition until whites form stiff peaks.

≈ Sprinkle lemon juice or vinegar, vanilla and coconut over whites. Gently fold in until just blended.

≈ Preheat oven to 300°F. Line 2 large cookie sheets with nonstick parchment paper or foil. Drop mixture by heaping teaspoonfuls, keeping a cone shape, about 1 inch apart.

≈ Bake 40–45 minutes until lightly browned; macaroons should be *very* slightly soft in center. Carefully peel off paper and cool completely. Store in an airtight container.

NUTRITION FACTS	
Amount per Serving (each)	
Calories 47	Calories from Fat 18
	% Daily Value
Total Fat 2g	3%
Saturated Fat 2g	10%
Polyunsaturated Fat 0.05g	0%
Monounsaturated Fat 0.1g	0%
Cholesterol 0mg	0%
Sodium 9mg	0.4%
Total Carbohydrate 7g	2%
Dietary Fiber 0.5g	2%
Sugars 7g	0%
Protein 0.5g	0%

Percent daily values are based on a 2000 calorie diet

EASY CINNAMON BALLS

MAKES ABOUT 20

These cookies are so easy children can make them. They should not go close to the oven and the size of the cookies will probably not be uniform, but they will have a good time. If mixture is too soft to roll, add a little more ground almond to stiffen it.

2 cups finely ground blanched
    almonds or walnuts
1 cup sugar
1 tbsp ground cinnamon
2 egg whites
⅛ tsp cream of tartar
confectioners' sugar and cinnamon
    for rolling

NUTRITION FACTS	
Amount per Serving (each)	
Calories 97	Calories from Fat 54
	% Daily Value
Total Fat 6g	9%
Saturated Fat 0.5g	2.5%
Polyunsaturated Fat 1g	0%
Monounsaturated Fat 3g	0%
Cholesterol 0mg	0%
Sodium 8mg	0.3%
Total Carbohydrate 10g	3%
Dietary Fiber 1g	4%
Sugars 10g	0%
Protein 2g	0%

Percent daily values are based on a 2000 calorie diet

≈ Preheat oven to 325°F. Lightly grease a large cookie sheet. In a medium bowl, combine ground almonds or walnuts, ½ cup sugar, and cinnamon. Set aside.
≈ In another medium bowl, with electric mixer, beat whites until frothy. Add cream of tartar and continue beating until soft peaks form. Gradually add remaining sugar, 1 tablespoonful at a time, beating well after each addition, until whites are stiff and glossy. Gently fold in nut mixture.

≈ With wet hands, shape mixture into walnut-size balls. Place on cookie sheet about 1-inch apart. Bake until golden brown and set, 25–30 minutes. Remove cookie sheet to wire rack to cool slightly.
≈ In a small bowl, combine ½ cup confectioners' sugar and ¼ teaspoon cinnamon until well blended. Roll each warm ball in mixture to coat, then set on wire rack to cool completely. Add more confectioners' sugar and cinnamon if necessary. When cold, roll each ball again in sugar mixture.

MUESLI COOKIES

MAKES 10

1 cup raisins
⅜ cup dried apricots, chopped
1 egg, beaten
2 tbsp polyunsaturated margarine,
    melted with 2 tbsp hot water
1½ cups muesli
1 heaped tbsp chopped nuts

NUTRITION FACTS	
Amount per Serving (per cookie)	
Calories 169	Calories from Fat 54
	% Daily Value
Total Fat 6g	9%
Saturated Fat 2g	10%
Polyunsaturated Fat 1g	0%
Monounsaturated Fat 02	0%
Cholesterol 30mg	10%
Sodium 192mg	8%
Total Carbohydrate 26g	9%
Dietary Fiber 3g	12%
Sugars 12g	0%
Protein 5g	0%

Percent daily values are based on a 2000 calorie diet

≈ Preheat the oven to 350°F.
≈ Pick over dried fruit and wash in boiling water. Drain. Put fruit in a bowl and beat well with egg and butter. Stir in muesli and nuts.
≈ Line a cookie tray with greased waxed paper and spread the mixture thinly over it. Mark into bars and bake for 45 minutes.

≈ Cut bars through and allow to cool for 10 minutes before removing from the tray. Finish cooling on a wire rack.

APPLE CAKE

SERVES 10

3 medium cooking apples, peeled,
    cored and sliced

a little cider

1 clove

2 tbsp polyunsaturated margarine

2 tbsp honey

2 tbsp molasses

1 egg

1 tsp mixed spice

pinch of salt

2 tsp baking powder

1 tsp baking soda

½ cup raisins

1½ cups whole-wheat flour

4 tbsp wheatgerm

1 tsp mixed spice

NUTRITION FACTS

Amount per Serving

Calories 131	Calories from Fat 27
	% Daily Value
Total Fat 3g	5%
Saturated Fat 0.5g	2.5%
Polyunsaturated Fat 1g	0%
Monounsaturated Fat 1g	0%
Cholesterol 24mg	8%
Sodium 29mg	1%
Total Carbohydrate 24g	8%
Dietary Fiber 3.5g	14%
Sugars 12g	0%
Protein 4g	0%

Percent daily values are based on a 2000 calorie diet

≈ Preheat the oven to 350°F.

≈ Poach the apple slices in a little cider with the clove until soft. Remove clove. Drain and reserve cider. Purée apples in a blender.

≈ In a large bowl mix margarine, honey, molasses and 1 tablespoon of reserved cider. Beat in egg. Stir in apples and remaining ingredients and mix well.

≈ Pour batter into a greased and floured loaf pan, 9 × 4 inches, and bake for about an hour until firm. Allow to stand for 10 minutes, then turn out of the pan and cool completely on a wire rack.

BRAN FRUIT LOAF

MAKES ONE 2 LB LOAF

It is always useful to have a moist fruit loaf on hand, especially at Christmas – this one keeps well in a tin cake box.

¾ cup 100% bran cereal

1¼ cups skimmed milk

1½ cups (scant) whole-wheat cake flour

1 tsp baking powder

1 tsp salt

¾ cup seedless raisins

⅓ cup currants

⅜ cup golden raisins

½ cup (scant) dark Muscovado or brown sugar

2 tbsp clear honey

2 tbsp molasses

oil, for brushing

≈ Soak the cereal in the milk for 30 minutes.

≈ Set the oven to 350°F. Sift together the flour, baking powder, and salt, and stir into the cereal mixture, together with any bran (husk) remaining in the sieve. Stir in the raisins, currants, sugar, honey, and molasses, and mix well.

≈ Lightly brush a 2-lb loaf pan with oil. Spoon in the cake mixture and level the top. Bake in the oven for 1–1¼ hours, until it is well-cooked and a skewer inserted in the center comes out clean.

≈ Allow the loaf to cool slightly in the pan, then turn it out to cool on a wire rack. When it is cool, wrap it in foil and store it in an airtight tin cake box.

NUTRITION FACTS	
Amount per Serving (per slice)	
Calories 135	Calories from Fat 5
	% Daily Value
Total Fat 0.5g	0.8%
Saturated Fat 0g	0%
Polyunsaturated Fat 0.2g	0%
Monounsaturated Fat 0g	0%
Cholesterol 0mg	0%
Sodium 61mg	2.5%
Total Carbohydrate 32g	11%
Dietary Fiber 3g	12%
Sugars 24g	0%
Protein 3g	0%

Percent daily values are based on a 2000 calorie diet

PUMPKIN, SUNFLOWER SEED, AND RAISIN CAKE

MAKES 10–12 SLICES

2¼ cups pumpkin

2¼ cups whole-wheat flour

pinch of salt

2 tsp baking powder

1 tsp baking soda

⅓ cup sunflower seeds, chopped

⅓ cup raisins

2 eggs

2 tbsp honey

2 tbsp molasses

1 tbsp warm water

NUTRITION FACTS	
Amount per Serving (per slice)	
Calories 126	Calories from Fat 36
	% Daily Value
Total Fat 4g	6%
Saturated Fat 0.5g	2.5%
Polyunsaturated Fat 2g	0%
Monounsaturated Fat 1g	0%
Cholesterol 40mg	13%
Sodium 18mg	0.75%
Total Carbohydrate 20g	7%
Dietary Fiber 3g	12%
Sugars 6g	0%
Protein 5g	0%

Percent daily values are based on a 2000 calorie diet

≈ Preheat the oven to 375°F. Peel the pumpkin, cut into smallish pieces and boil until tender. Drain and cut up finely.

≈ Combine flour, salt, baking powder, sunflower seeds, and raisins and mix well.

≈ In another bowl, beat the eggs and stir in the honey and molasses. Add 1 tablespoon of warm water with the pumpkin and beat well.

≈ Mix all the ingredients together thoroughly and pour into a greased and floured pan. Bake for 50–60 minutes until done. Allow to stand for 10 minutes in the pan, then cool on a wire rack.

BANANA, NECTARINE, AND ALMOND LOAF

MAKES 10–12 SLICES

2 cups whole-wheat flour

½ cup wheatgerm

¼ cup dried nectarines, chopped

¼ cup almonds, chopped

2 tsp baking powder

1 tsp baking soda

pinch of salt

2 tbsp honey

2 tbsp molasses

½ tsp vanilla

3 bananas, mashed

1 egg, beaten

≈ Preheat the oven to 350°F.

≈ Mix the dry ingredients together in a large bowl. Mix the remaining ingredients together thoroughly in another bowl, then combine the two and stir well.

≈ Tip into a greased and floured loaf pan 9 × 4 inches, and bake for about 50 minutes, or until a toothpick inserted in the middle of the loaf comes out cleanly. Allow to cool for 15 minutes, then tip out of the pan and cool completely on a wire rack before cutting. Eat it on its own or spread it with low-fat spread or cream cheese.

NUTRITION FACTS	
Amount per Serving (per slice)	
Calories 134	Calories from Fat 27
	% Daily Value
Total Fat 3g	5%
Saturated Fat 0.5g	2.5%
Polyunsaturated Fat 1g	0%
Monounsaturated Fat 1.5g	0%
Cholesterol 20mg	7%
Sodium 10mg	0.4%
Total Carbohydrate 23g	8%
Dietary Fiber 4g	16%
Sugars 10g	0%
Protein 5g	0%

Percent daily values are based on a 2000 calorie diet

CARROT AND ORANGE CAKE

MAKES 10–12 SLICES

2 tbsp oil

2 tbsp honey

2 tbsp molasses

2 eggs

2–2½ cups carrot, peeled and grated

grated rind of one orange

1 tbsp orange juice

2¼ cups whole-wheat flour

4 tbsp wheatgerm

1 tsp cinnamon

pinch of salt

2 tsp baking powder

1 tsp baking soda

NUTRITION FACTS

Amount per Serving (per slice (¹⁄₁₂))

Calories 114	Calories from Fat 36
	% Daily Value
Total Fat 4g	6%
Saturated Fat 0.5g	2.5%
Polyunsaturated Fat 2g	0%
Monounsaturated Fat 1g	0%
Cholesterol 40mg	13%
Sodium 21mg	1%
Total Carbohydrate 17g	6%
Dietary Fiber 3.5g	14%
Sugars 4g	0%
Protein 4g	0%

Percent daily values are based on a 2000 calorie diet

≈ Preheat oven to 375°F.

≈ Beat together the oil, honey, molasses, and eggs. Stir in the carrot, orange rind, and juice.

≈ Combine the dry ingredients in a bowl and stir in the carrot mixture. Mix well. Pour into a greased and floured 9-inch cake pan.

≈ Bake for about 30 minutes or until done. Cool for 10 minutes in the pan, then remove and cool completely on a wire rack.

INDEX